PERSPECTIVES ON THE NURTURING OF FAITH

Leland Harder,
Editor

Occasional Papers

No. 6

The Institute of Mennonite Studies

3003 Benham Avenue

Elkhart, Indiana 46517

1983

POLICY STATEMENT FOR THE *OCCASIONAL PAPERS*

Occasional Papers is a publication of the Institute of Mennonite
Studies and authorized by the Council of Mennonite Seminaries.
The four sponsoring seminaries are Eastern Mennonite Seminary
(Harrisonburg, VA), Goshen Biblical Seminary and Mennonite Biblical
Seminary (Elkhart, IN), and the Mennonite Brethren Biblical Seminary
(Fresno, CA). The Institute of Mennonite Studies is the research
agency of the Associated Mennonite Biblical Seminaries.

Occasional Papers is released several times yearly without any
prescribed calendar schedule. The purpose of the *Papers* is to
make various types of essays available for critical counsel from
within the Mennonite theological community. While most essays
will be in finished form, some may also be in a more germinal
stage--released especially for purposes of testing and receiving
critical feedback. In accepting papers for publication, priority
will be given to authors from the CMS institutions, the College
Bible faculties in the Council of Mennonite Colleges, the
Associate membership of the Institute of Mennonite Studies, and
students and degree alumni of the four seminaries.

Because of the limited circulation of the *Occasional Papers*,
authors are free to use their material in other scholarly settings,
either for oral presentation at scholarly meetings or for publication in journals with broader circulation and more official
publication policies.

The price for *Occasional Papers* is $5.00 per copy. Make checks
payable to the Institute of Mennonite Studies. Orders and articles
for publication should be sent to the Institute of Mennonite Studies,
3003 Benham Avenue, Elkhart, IN 46517

Editors: Willard M. Swartley, Director
            Institute of Mennonite Studies
          Leland Harder, Associate Director
            Institute of Mennonite Studies

PERSPECTIVES ON THE NURTURING OF FAITH

Contents

EDITOR'S PREFACE

The Seminar-Workshop on Congregational Education
which produced the papers, responses, discussions, and
findings included in this book, was held at the Associated Mennonite Biblical Seminaries in March 1982. The
role of moderating that seminar was bequeathed to me by
the Director of the Institute of Mennonite Studies, who
was on sabbatical in Europe. The memoranda in his file
spanned over three years of prior planning that led to
the gathering of over fifty participants whose names are
listed on pages 14-16.

The term "nurture" used in the title of this book is
intended as a synonym for congregational education in a
meaning more inclusive than its more commonly delimited
connotations of a largely unconscious and informal
assimilation of beliefs and attitudes of faith through
natural kinds of associations with devout parents and
congregational mentors. As the papers and discussions
indicate, the seminar participants were not willing to
settle for a restrictive definition or model, although
neither were they wanting to abandon the search for an
integrative holistic conception of the church's teaching
ministry. So pending further clarification, the many
references herein to "the nuturing of faith" embrace
formal schooling, informal fosterage, personal experience
and participation, conversion and voluntary discipleship.

This book is itself a blend of the "formal" and "informal" components of education. The responses to each
paper, the plenary discussions, the small group report-
backs, and the observor reports of the listening team,
were gleaned from over 100 typewritten pages of transcription of tape recordings of the proceedings of those
three days. The editor is indebted to the IMS secretary,
Rachel Lehman Stoltzfus, not only for overseeing the
arduous process of recording and transcribing, but also
for attending to many of the administrative details of

seminar and typing most of the copy-ready manuscript for printing before she and Eldon and their children left for their mission assignment in Haiti. What she could not finish was ably typed by the present IMS secretary, Emilie Seitz.

It has been my challenging responsibility to excerpt and edit the spontaneous oral comments of selected participants, hopefully without straying too far from the transcription, and in any case with apologies to participants who may wonder whether they really said those things.

It was a special privilege to work with the members of the task force who planned and engineered the whole event--John Gaeddert, who administered the Mennonite Mutual Aid Association fraternal grant that subsidized the travel expenses of participants and other costs; David Helmuth, who supervised their various meetings, including the post-seminar session to rewrite the statement of findings; Herta Funk, who wrote the minutes of that session; Laurence Martin, who worked at prior drafts and led some congregational "testings" of the "assumptions and implications" found herein; and Ross Bender, my AMBS colleague who wrote the prospectus for the seminar and was really its suffering servant catalyst from beginning to end.

Leland Harder
May 10, 1983

INTRODUCTION

Ross T. Bender

The vision for a seminar-workshop on congregational education emerged out of a series of conversations over a period of several years. Participants in the conversation were John Gaeddert of the General Conference Mennonite Commission on Education, Newton, KS; David Helmuth of the Mennonite Board of Congregational Ministries, Elkhart, IN; Laurence Martin of the Congregational Literature Division of Mennonite Publishing House, Scottdale, PA; and Ross T. Bender of the Associated Mennonite Biblical Serminaries, Elkhart, IN. These conversations focused on finding ways to energize and give direction to the teaching ministry of the church in the context of the congregation.

It was noted that the mission agencies of the church in cooperation with the AMBS Institute of Mennonite Studies had found a vehicle for bringing persons into vigorous conversation around the contemporary missions agenda through annual sessions of the Mennonite Missionary Study Fellowship. These sessions had resulted in the publication of papers which brought a wider group of persons into the conversation and debate. Willard Swartley, the newly appointed director of the Institute agreed to arrange for a similar seminar-workshop in cooperation with the Christian education agencies of the two sponsoring Mennonite bodies. The sessions were held on the AMBS campus, March 23-25, 1982, under the capable administrative leadership of the IMS Associate Director, Leland Harder.

Over fifty persons were present to listen and
respond to the papers and to engage in stimulating discussion of the issues they raised. The stated purpose
of the seminar-workshop was "to develop a new model
of Christian education consonant with the biblical and
believer's church model of intergenerational transmittal
of faith learnings and values."

Much of the debate was provoked by the bias of the
planning committee in setting up the seminar around a
focal concept. The statement in the prospectus was
as follows:

> The focal concept which we propose to
> research and test is that of the faith com-
> munity as the guiding image for nurturing
> faith. What we are searching for is an
> approach which is most faithful to our bib-
> lical/historical heritage as well as most
> effective in shaping our educational efforts
> in the congregation in coming years. While
> we do not reject nor disparage the educa-
> tional model of the school, we are increas-
> ingly questioning whether the things that
> schooling does most effectively are adequate
> instruments for achieving the distinctive
> goals and dealing with the distinctive
> content of the educational ministry of the
> congregation. We refer to such things as
> the emphasis on cognitive learning, the
> grading principle, developmental tasks,
> teachers and learners, classes, lessons,
> etc. It is not that we believe such consid-
> erations are irrelevant to the congrega-
> tion's educational ministry, but that they
> ought not occupy the central place in
> curricular design and educational assumptions
> they have come to hold!

> If we are serious about schooling, we
> ought to set up the structures which make

authentic schooling possible that is to say, a total system of schools in which the three R's and the fourth R (Religion) are not divorced from each other. We believe that it is not an adequate response to the need for that kind of integration nor, for that matter, to the need for cognitive mastery of the Christian heritage to devote one hour (or less) on Sunday morning to study it and to call that limited effort a school.

It is not, however, a call to a more rigorous schooling program that we are raising but a call to consider a fundamentally different approach in the congregation. Where considerations such as transmission of content, developmental stages, grading, etc., become significant, they will be incorporated into the design. They will not, however, become the organizing principle nor the building blocks of the proposed new approach in which "faith community" rather than "school" becomes the basic paradigm.

Schooling is a relatively recent phenomenon in congregational Christian education. For generations, other approaches to nurturing faith were employed with great effectiveness. It is significant to note that time and again in the history of God's people, formal educational approaches (schools) began to displace informal ones (families) when the vitality of the original faith began to fade. When the culture surrounding the growing child became less supportive of the religious values and practices which were to be inculcated, the people began schools and raised up teachers who took up what was formerly the responsibility of the parents.

While the proposed model does not call for the abolition of schools, it does make a fundamentally different assumption--that the basic responsibility for nurturing faith rests with the parents and the families of the church. The school model tends to say that the school and the teachers carry that responsibility and that parents and families are called upon to *support* that effort and *cooperate* with it. Sometimes the assumption (implicit or explicit) is that families by and large are too busy or too incompetent to be entrusted with even this limited responsibility. In response to the objection that the proposed reversal of the focus of responsibility is overly demanding on the family, we reply that no educational program with minimal expectations of the family can be effective.

Characteristics of the Proposed Design

We propose an educational design as the *core curriculum* emphasis which has the following characteristics:

- extended family
- inter-generational
- inclusive (male/female; single/ married; older/younger; rural/ urban; multi-ethnic)
- active participation of parents and children a central assumption
- local initiative in curriculum planning is required
- action/reflection as a basic method
- storytelling an important medium; use of story books
- informal settings (homes)
- emphasis on relationships

- modeling (in word and deed,
  in life)
- biblical materials a central
  resource informing the present
  life of God's people in the
  world
- intra-generational spiritual
  renewal, recommitment, recov-
  enanting

We are hoping to design a model which

a) is not limited to the second
   hour on Sunday morning, but
   will break that mold;
b) does not assume existing resources of buildings, facili-
   ties, materials, but is flexible for use in a variety of
   settings (rural, urban, inner
   city) and a diversity of life
   situations;
c) has the capacity to reshape
   not only our educational program, but also our congregational life and our family life.

The plan had been to set up a task force to work on
a new curricular design which would incorporate such
elements as those outlined above. The traditional curricular questions of context, scope, purpose, process
and organizing principle were to be re-examined in a new
way with the assumptions outlined in the focal concept.
A number of other persons were to be asked to prepare
and present written critiques of the proposed design. A
major block of time was to have been devoted to critical
analysis of the design by all participants with a view
to modifying or rejecting it.

Even before the seminar convened, however, objections began to be raised to this procedure. One invitee
declined to come to a conference "where the conclusions

have already been stated before the conference even
begins." Some staff persons in the participating agencies expressed strong reservations both about the assumptions and the procedures. Various expressions of dissent
were heard throughout the several days of the seminar
though it was never entirely clear whether the objections were addressed to the proposed procedures or to
the assumptions in the focal concept which were to be
tested.

In any event, due to a variety of circumstances
including conflicting schedules and stormy winter
weather, the task force was unable to meet in advance to
carry out its assignment. There was no model to expose
to critical analysis apart from the skeletal outline in
the prospectus.

There were a number of well-prepared papers on the
theme of the nurturing of faith (see Table of Contents).
This theme was explored in biblical perspective (Old
Testament, New Testament and Patristic periods), in historical perspective (Medieval era, among the Anabaptists
and the Mennonites), and in cross-cultural perspective
(Black and Hispanic; a hoped-for paper on Native American perspectives did not materialize). Four persons
responded to each presentation. In addition, there were
small group and plenary discussions. One highlight of
the seminar was the report of a congregational listening
team from the Berkey Avenue Fellowship. Another highlight was the morning worship in the chapel led each day
by Rebecca Slough.

While the seminar-workshop did not result in
designing a new model, it did result in consensus on ten
basic understandings which are included in this report.
A number of educational implications which follow from
these basic understandings are also spelled out. These
basic understandings and educational implications are
being tested with congregational educational leaders in
various places across the church. It is hoped that the
feedback from these soundings will be available for a

second seminar-workshop to be held sometime in the not-too-distant future.

This report, edited by Leland Harder, now goes to a wider group of participants with the invitation to join in an ongoing conversation about the issues it raises. The nurturing of faith is a continuing task to which we must bring the highest qualities of mind, heart and spirit of which we are capable.

Ross T. Bender
Professor of Christian Education
Associated Mennonite Biblical Seminaries
Elkhart, Indiana
May 5, 1983

SEMINAR PERSONNEL

Augsburger, Donald--Professor of Work of the Church, Eastern Mennonite Seminary, Harrisonburg, Virginia

Bauman, Harold--Associate Secretary for Congregational Leadership, Mennonite Board of Congregational Ministries, Elkhart, Indiana

Bender, Ross--Professor of Christian Education, Associated Mennonite Biblical Seminaries, Elkhart, Indiana

Berry, Elizabeth Ann Hostetler--formerly chairperson of the Nurture Committee, Berkey Avenue Fellowship and Assistant Professor of Education, Goshen College, Goshen, Indiana

Brunk, George R. III--Dean and Professor of New Testament, Eastern Mennonite Seminary, Harrisonburg, Pennsylvania

Casas, Arnoldo--Associate Secretary for the Spanish Curriculum Project, Mennonite Board of Congregational Ministries, Elkhart, Indiana

Cressman, David--Marketing Manager, Congregational Literature Division, Mennonite Publication Board, Scottdale, Pennsylvania

Derstine, Mark--Pastor, Blooming Glen, Pennsylvania, Mennonite Church

Dunn, James--Director of Higher Education, Commission on Education, General Conference Mennonite Church, Newton, Kansas

Dyck, C. J.--Professor of Anabaptist and Sixteenth Century Studies, Associated Mennonite Biblical Seminaries, Elkhart, Indiana

Dyck, Edna--Revision Editor of the Foundation Series, Commission on Education, General Conference Mennonite Church, Newton, Kansas

Erb, Peter C.--Professor of English and Religion and Culture, Wilfrid Laurier University, Waterloo, Ontario

Falcon, A. Rafael--Director of Hispanic Ministries Department and Assistant Professor of Spanish, Goshen College, Goshen, Indiana

Funk, Herta--Director of Adult Education, Commission on Education, General Conference Mennonite Church, Newton, Kansas

Gaeddert, John--Executive Secretary, Commission on Education, General Conference Mennonite Church, Newton, Kansas

Geiser, Linea--Member, Commission on Congregational Education and Literature, Mennonite Board of Congregational Ministries, and revision editor for 5th and 6th grade Foundation Series

Harder, Bertha--Lecturer in Christian Education, Associated Mennonite Biblical Seminaries, Elkhart, Indiana

Harder, Helmut--Professor of Theology, Canadian Mennonite Bible College, Winnipeg, Manitoba, and Executive Director, Foundation Series for Youth and Adults

Harder, Leland--Professor of Practical Theology and Associate Director of the Institute of Mennonite Studies, Associated Mennonite Biblical Seminaries, Elkhart, Indiana

Horsch, James--Editor, *Mennonite Yearbook*, Mennonite Publication Board, Scottdale, Pennsylvania

Hostetler, Marvin--Middler Student, Associated Mennonite Biblical Seminaries and member of the Vision Committee, Berkey Avenue Fellowship, Goshen, Indiana

Janzen, Dorothea--Co-Pastor, Trinity Mennonite Church, Hillsboro, Kansas, and member of the Board of Trustees, Mennonite Biblical Seminary, Hillsboro, Kansas

Janzen, Waldemar--Professor of Old Testament, Canadian Mennonite Bible College, Winnipeg, Manitoba

Kauffman, Norman--Dean of Student Development, Dean of Student Services and Assistant Professor of Psychology, Goshen College, Goshen, Indiana

Kennel, LeRoy E.--Professor of Communications, Bethany Theological Seminary, Oak Brook, Illinois, and Former Associate Director Chicago Area Ministries

Kennel, Pauline--Former Director of Christian Education, Yorkfield Presbyterian Church, Elmhurst, Illinois, and presently Coordinator, Chicago Area Mennonites

Konrad, George--Professor of Christian Education, Mennonite Brethren Biblical Seminary, Fresno, California, and author of Foundation Series for Adult study book, *Living as God's Family*

Kropf, Marlene--Mennonite congregational educator, Portland, Oregon, member of the Council on Faith, Life and Strategy of the Mennonite Church General Board

Lehn, Cornelis--Formerly Director of Children's Education, Commission on Education, General Conference Mennonite Church, Newton, Kansas, author of children's books, and presently retired to her home in Chilliwack, British Columbia.

Loewen, Eleanor--Education Consultant and Director of the Resource Centre, Congregational Resources Board, Conference of Mennonites in Canada, Winnipeg, Manitoba

Martin, Laurence--Director, Division of Congregational Literature, Mennonite Publication Board, Scottdale, Pennsylvania

Miller, Donald E.--Professor of Christian Education and Ethics and Director of Graduate Studies, Bethany Theological Seminary, Oak Brook, Illinois

Miller, Levi--Associate Editor, Congregation Literature Division, Mennonite Publication Board, on 2-year leave in Caracus, Venezuela

Rempel, Dietrich--Director, Faith and Life Press, General Conference Mennonite Church, Newton, Kansas

Reusser, Helen--Co-Pastor, Mannheim Mennonite Church, Kitchener, Ontario, and Christian Education Consultant, Ontario Mennonite Conference

Rogers, John A.--Editor, *Builder* and The Foundation Series for Youth and Adults, Mennonite Publication Board, Scottdale, Pennsylvania

Rupp, Anne--Co-Pastor, Alexanderwohl Mennonite Church, Goessel, Kansas

Schrag, James--Pastor, Tabor Mennonite Church, Rural Route 2, Newton, Kansas and Chairman of the Western District Conference Education Committee

Slough, Rebecca--Graduate student in Worship, Divinity School, University of Notre Dame, South Bend, Indiana

Smoker, Arthur E.--Pastor, Berkey Avenue Fellowship, Goshen, Indiana

Swalm, Winnie--Executive Director, Board of Christian Education, Brethren in Christ Church

Suderman, Alice--Chairperson, Commission on Education, General Conference Mennonite Church, Newton, Kansas, and congregational educator, Bethel Mennonite Church, Mountain Lake, Minnesota

Unruh, Paul--Co-Director of Marriage Encounter Seminars, Commission on Education, General Conference Mennonite Church, Newton, Kansas

Waybill, Marjorie--Associate Editor of Children's Curriculum, *Rejoice*, *Story Friends*, and the Foundation Series for Children

Welty, Lavon--Associate Secretary for Congregational Youth Ministries, Mennonite Board of Congregational Ministries, Elkhart, Indiana

Yoder, Elizabeth--General Editor, Commission on Education, General Conference Mennonite Church, Newton, Kansas

Zook, Gordon--Executive Secretary and Director of Development, Mennonite Board of Congregational Ministries, Elkhart, Indiana

OLD TESTAMENT AND EARLY
JUDAISTIC PERSPECTIVES*

Waldemar Janzen

I.

Education as we think of it was unknown in Old
Testament Israel. No school system existed, although
some scholars claim that literacy was widespread.[1]
Learning did take place, however, and at times, perhaps, in ways less lost in massive educational bu-
reaucracies and more appropriate to the needs of the
people than ours today.

What else is education than "a conversation between generations?" I heard this definition years ago,
and I do believe that it describes well the heart and
soul of that vast realm of endeavors. The Old Testament offers us some very basic models of such conversation, models that are effective today also, but
can be seen more clearly in their forthright simplicity
in Old Testament times. They are models of parent and
child, wise man and "fool," master and disciple, and
priest and member of the congregation of Israel.

1. Parent and Child. This is the primary learning relationship among all peoples, and even among
many animals. Such learning begins at birth, and for
the Israelite son or daughter, who continued to live
in the context of the "father's house" (*bêt'âb*) or
extended family,[2] it had no formal conclusion. The
"curriculum" of this schooling consisted of the things
needful to know for the survival and flourishing of
the individual and the social group. A distinction
between learning and work, such as we know, did not
exist. Learning was largely imitation by doing. As

*This paper had advance publication as Chapter 10 in
Waldemar Janzen's, *Still in the Image* (Newton: Faith
and Life Press, 1982), in the IMS Study Series.

children outgrew the first infant years, boys imi-
tated the ways of their father and the other men, while
girls watched their mother and the other women. Life
in Old Testament Israel was not prudishly segregated,
however.

Adulthood was marked for the man by the right to
participate in four great orders of life: marriage,
justice, warfare, and cultus.[3] A girl achieved
womanhood through marriage and child-bearing. Exact
ages and specific ceremonies of passage are not reported to us.[4] And we should remember that the
achievement of such marks of adulthood did not mean
economic, vocational or social "independence," as we
think of it, for the young man remained a part of his
father's house, while the young woman joined the
father's house of her husband.

"Religious education" was not set apart as a
separate compartment of learning.

When your son asks you in time to come,
'What is the meaning of the testimonies
and the statutes and the ordinances which
the Lord our God has commanded you?' then
you shall say to your son, 'We were
Pharaoh's slaves in Egypt; and the Lord
brought us out of Egypt. . .'

In this way the classical statement in Deuteronomy
6:20-21 incorporates religious education into the
everyday conversation between parent and child (Ex.
10:2, 12:26-27; 13:8; Deut. 4:9; 6:7; 32:7, 46). We
can be sure that such learning was considered just
as important for individual and group survival as the
arts of ploughing the field, grinding flour, or making
a garment. And in this area, perhaps even more than
in other realms of life, learning remained open-ended,
for father and mother also continued to learn from the
priests and the sages, as we shall see shortly.[5]

2. <u>Wise man and "Fool."</u> The individual household
was embedded in the <u>clan</u> (*mishpāhāh*) or <u>village</u>. This
expanded social context offered further scope for
learning. L. Koehler has given us a masterful description of the ancient Israelite "village circle"
(*sod*).[6] It was the gathering of the men of the
village after the day's work was done, while the
women and girls were still occupied with the household chores. One would meet under a big tree, or at
the well, or at the open place by the gate. No one
was forced to come, but everyone wanted to be there,
to enjoy the fellowship, to exchange the news of the
day, to hear the stories of someone just back from
a journey, to sing the familiar songs and, last but
not least, to engage in that mental activity which
we may call "popular wisdom" or "folk wisdom," in
contrast to its more sophisticated relative called
"court wisdom."

The village circle is the life setting of many
of such proverbs and riddles as we find in the book
of Proverbs, beginning with chapter 10. After the
bustle of news exchange had settled down, one of the
elders might raise his voice:

A glad heart makes a cheerful countenance.

This was a challenge which another was quick to take
up:

But by sorrow of heart the spirit is broken.
(Prov. 15:13).

Then another voice:

A wise son makes a glad father.

And the reply out of the darkness of the evening:

But a foolish son is a sorrow to his mother.
(Prov. 10:1).

And another challenge:

> Three things are too wonderful for me; four I
> do not understand.

After some silence, a voice might venture forth with
a first answer:

> The way of an eagle in the sky.

A second voice:

> The way of a serpent on a rock.

A third voice:

> The way of a ship on the high seas.

Then, finally, the clincher:

> And the way of a man with a maiden. (Prov. 30:18-
> 19)

This could go on and on. The old men took the
lead, but from time to time a younger voice from the
outer edges of the circle would dare to make itself
heard.

Of course, such proverbs were not always made up
on the spot. They were transmitted from generation
to generation, and each encapsuled in its terse form
the results of long and perceptive observation of the
patterns and interrelationships placed into life by
God. In a sense, this wisdom, based on empirical observation, constituted the Israelites' natural and
social sciences. There is one difference, however.
While our sciences formulate into laws what must
always happen in the controlled environment of an ex-
periment, the proverbs of the wise put in focus what
will *often* happen in the less controlled setting of
daily life. That is the difference between wisdom and
science.

Much of this wisdom was "secular," by our definition, dealing with wealth and poverty, work and
leisure, neighbourly relations, marriage, agriculture,
etc. But again, the religious sphere is not separated
from daily life. The wise knew well that human observation was limited in its capacity to understand
the world. They acknowledged the mystery of God's
ways:

Many are the plans in the mind of a man,
but it is the purpose of the Lord that will
be established. (Prov. 19:21)

Further, they taught righteous living:

Better is a little with righteousness
than great revenues with injustice. (Prov.
16:8)

But the real religious significance of this education
lay not in explicitly religious statements like
these, but in the assumption underlying all wisdom,
namely that it is based on observation of the order   X
of God's world. And by including such proverbs, the
Old Testament acknowledges that revelation of God can
indeed come through empirical observation.

3. Priest and Member of the Congregation of
Israel. The educational setting of the ancient
Israelite extended beyond the family and the village
circle, however, to include the sanctuaries staffed
by the professional teachers, the priests.[8] While we
often associate priests primarily with sacrifices and
liturgical acts, we must not overlook the fact that
their other chief function in Israel was to be
guardians and dispensers of tôrāh, i.e. instruction.
Deuteronomy 33:10 summarizes their dual commission:

They (the Levites, i.e. the priestly
tribe) shall teach Jacob thy ordinances,
and Israel thy law;
they shall put incense before thee,
and whole burnt offering upon thy altar.

Their special guardianship of *tôrāh* is also stated clearly in Mic. 3:11; Jer. 18:18; and Ezek. 7:26.

Tôrāh may be derived from the verb *yārāh*, "to throw," and even "to cast lots" (Josh. 18:6). It may thus be related to the giving of oracles. However, its Old Testament usage suggests that it derives rather from the root *yārāh*, "to show, teach," so that its original meaning is "instruction."[9] Its usual translation as "law," though fixed by long tradition, is hardly appropriate for the Old Testament period itself and obscures the basic teaching function of the priests.

For the longest stretch of Israel's existence in her land, such teaching was concentrated at the Temple in Jerusalem. Three times a year every Israelite male was required to "appear before the Lord" (Ex. 23:14-17; 34:18-23; Deut. 16; Lev. 23; Num. 28-29), i.e. make a pilgrimage to the place where the Ark of the Covenant was kept. We can be sure that this requirement was fulfilled only symbolically, as some persons and families from across the land made the pilgrimage. For some, it may have been the desire of their lifetime to set foot inside the Temple at least once. Nevertheless, the Temple was the goal of pilgrimages on the part of many people on the occasion of the three great pilgrim feasts: Passover/Unleavened Bread; Harvest/Weeks; and Ingathering/Booths, held in early Spring, at Mid-Summer, and in late Fall, respectively (30:29; Ps. 122; cf. Luke 2:11-51).

These feasts lasted for eight days each. They were marked by great liturgical events in which the whole congregation participated. At these high points the great acts of God in Israel's history must have been recited and celebrated, such as the exodus from Egypt, the crossing of the Sea, the preservation in the wilderness, the occupation of the land under Joshua, and the election of David. Such celebration, with its recitals and symbols, was in itself highly educational.

During the festal week, however, there must have been many occasions for instruction in smaller groups. H. Kraus postulates that such instruction must have pertained to two areas: Yahweh's Torah and Yahweh's acts in creation and history.[10] He considers Ps. 119 to be the most impressive document of Torah-instruction. Study of this sort may have been carried on in small groups. Kraus proposes the further interesting theory that the seven-day account of creation (Gen. 1) might have corresponded to seven days of the festivals in such a way that the works of one day of creation may have been studied on each day of a festival week, accompanied by psalms such as Ps. 8.[11] The acts of God in Israel's history were surely told and retold, again accompanied by psalms, such as Ps. 105; 135; and 136, for poetry and song were important teaching devices (Deut. 31:19), as were the symbols of the Temple's structure and its liturgies.

Whatever were the details, we must assume that the pilgrim feasts were significant "short-courses" in religion, not to mention the general educational value of a trip to Jerusalem and an encounter with many people from all parts of the land. Private trips to the Temple on other occasions will also have taken place. At the centre of such education stood the priests. That their teaching function was seen as a "conversation between the generations," in analogy to the parents' role, is shown by the occasional use of the term "father" for them (Judg. 17:10; 18:19).[12]

4. <u>Master and Disciple</u>. Until now we have considered forms of education to which all or most Israelites were exposed. Now we must turn to what we might call exclusive and specialized education. Most people in Israel were peasants and/or shepherds or herdsmen, even if they lived in towns. They learned their skills by observing their parents and neighbours, as we have seen above. There were some vocations requiring special skills, however, and such skills were acquired in a sort of apprenticeship to someone accomplished in them, a master.

Earlier we considered "folk wisdom," dealing with various life issues on the basis of accumulated experience. Learning by observation could also take place with respect to a particular and limited area of life, such as pottery making, carpentry, midwifery, etc.[13] A person accomplished in such specialities was called "wise" (*ḥākām*). Our Bible translations render the word, if used in this context, as "able" or "skilled," but it is important to note that there is continuity of designation between those "skilled" in various crafts and those "wise" men and women who coined our proverbs. Craftmen's skills were learned, as we said already, from experienced masters. There is some evidence that there were guilds in Israel.[14] Often a skill will have been handed down in a family, so that the master-disciple relationship coincided with that of parent and child. But this was surely not always the case. The head of a guild was called "father" (I Chron. 4:14), showing once again how the parent-child pattern was the basic model of learning.[15]

The priesthood was hereditary. It required extensive training. Little is reported of this, but we must assume that certain older priests will have instructed the younger ones in the sacred lore of Israel and in such matters as are recorded in the book of Leviticus. From an earlier time we have the story of Samuel's apprenticeship to the priest Eli (I Sam. 1-3). In 2 Kings 12:3 we have the interesting note that the priest Jehoiada "instructed" the young king Jehoash who began to reign when he was seven years old. Thus it appears that priests may have given instruction even to some outside of the priestly lineage on a one-to-one basis.

A variety of special skills, from writing to statecraft and diplomacy, were required by the royal court and the government service. Thus the royal court became a centre of the particular kind of learning which we may call "court wisdom," in contrast to "folk wisdom" and to the wisdom or skill of craftsmen. It has been suggested that there were formal schools for scribes at the royal courts of Samaria and Jerusalem, on the analogy to such schools in Egypt, Mesopotamia, and elsewhere. However, there is no explicit evidence for this.

Nevertheless, kings had their "wise men" as advisers (1 Sam. 16:15-17:23), and these undoubtedly had their disciples whom they trained in the arts of writing, statecraft, and diplomacy, but also in proper etiquette and in wise behaviour at court (cf. Prov. 16:10-15). The young kings themselves were in need of such training and will have had their special mentors, as mentioned in connection with Johoash and Jehoiada above. Joseph fulfilled such a role toward Pharaoh and is consequently called a "father to Pharaoh" (Gen. 45:8). That the king himself could become a wise man is best illustrated by Solomon, the "patron saint" of wisdom in the Old Testament (1 Kings 3; 4:29-34). Through such activity the royal court became a centre of learning, a higher academy, so to speak, where wise men (and women?) taught, but also preserved the wisdom handed down (Prov. 25:1).

Finally, we know that the master-disciple relationship existed in the realm of the prophets. Elijah had his disciple Elisha (2 Kings 2), who in turn had Gehasi (e.g. 2 Kings 4:11ff), and was generally seen as a father figure by the "sons of the prophets" (e.g. 2 Kings 6:1-7). Perhaps the clearest example of a master-disciple relationship is that between Jeremiah and Baruch (ef. Jer. 36; cf. also Is. 8:16). Characteristically, the master is called "father" in various such contexts (2 Kings 2: 12; 13:14), for learning in Israel, as now, is a conversation between the generations.

II.

If education in the Old Testament is a conversation between generations proceeding in four exemplary models, the question concerning the dynamics and the mood of such interchange must arise. Was there a smooth and peaceful flow of learning from the older generation to the younger, or was intergenerational communication marked by frustration, rebelliousness, and erratic results?[16]

In order to respond to this question, we must first define more closely who the teaching and the learning generations were. Of the four educational models discussed, only the parent-child model involved young children in a significant way. The other three models approximated more closely what we would call adult education, granted that adulthood began relatively early in ancient Israel. J. Conrad, in the only extensive study of youth in the Old Testament known to me,[17] draws the significant intergenerational boundary between "the young generation," which has not yet assumed its full significance in upholding society, and the "older generation," consisting of those who carry the full responsibility for the life of the community. In other words, the "young generation" is marked by its "unfinished, becoming" quality and must be seen in terms of the *telos* or goal towards which it is developing.[18]

1. Conrad delineates three perspectives on the goals of the young generation.[19] From the traditional perspective of the patriarchally structured clans, the young generation was valued as the carrier of the clan's biological and social future. This value was achieved simply by being, without any educational aims and achievements. Of course, it was taken for granted that children and young people would acquire the skills necessary for living and practice these diligently.

On the whole, we can assume that young people sub-
mitted rather matter-of-factly to the authority of
parents and elders and accepted readily their traditional skills, values, and way of life, including their
religious faith. After all, an individual did not
have any real alternative as to lifestyle in a homo-
geneous clan-centered society. While the prophets
warned continually against a deviation from God's ways
on the part of the people, there was little danger
that individuals would break away from the norms of
society. Disobedience on the part of children did not
have that ominous and forboding quality which it ac-
quires in our pluralistic society, and father's firm
hand was enough to deal with it effectively (Prov.
23:13f.; 29:15). There was legal provision for a
communally imposed death sentence against a "rebellious
son" (Deut. 21:18-21). Such a situation must have been
very exceptional, however, and no instance of an actual
verdict to this effect is reported to us.

There must have been serious tensions between the
generations, however, as is evidenced by the repeated
commandments and exhortations to treat parents properly
(Ex. 20:12; 21:15; Prov. 28:24; 30:17). Kings were in
a better position to express their individuality, and
consequently we witness many sharp contrasts in the
policies, lifestyles and religious attitudes of
fathers and sons of the royal house of David (cf. the
drastic contrasts as we move from father to son among
these kings: Ahaz, Hezekiah, Mannasseh and Amon,
Josiah, Jehoiakim). The disturbed social conditions
after the fall of Jerusalem and in the Babylonian
exile may have widened the scope of individual self-
expression for many Jews (Ezek. 18).

On the whole, however, the assertion of the young
against their elders was seen not only as wrong and
counterproductive (Ex. 20:12; Prov. 15:5, 32; 17:25;
28:24; 30:17; etc.), but as a sign of Divine judgment
(Is. 3:4-5; Mic. 7:6). The destructive course of
listening to the advice of the young and disregarding
that of the old is graphically described in 1 Kings 12,

leading to the division of the kingdom of Solomon.[20]
It belongs to the possibilities of the sinful present
order, while the restoration of harmony between the
generations will be a mark of the coming Day of the
Lord, when the new Elijah will "turn the hearts of
fathers to their children and the hearts of children
to their father" (Mal. 4:5-6; cf. 1 Kings 18:37).

2. From an educational perspective, presupposed
already in the commandment to honour father and mother
(Ex. 20:12), but particularly evident in the wisdom
tradition, the aim and goal of the younger generation
was to lead the good, wise and pious life (Prov. 1:7).
The easy achievement of this ideal could not be taken
for granted. The very fervour with which the wisdom
teachers propagated the life of wisdom and warned of
the life of folly (Prov. 1-9) shows that the younger
generation (addressed in fatherly terms as "My son!";
cf. Prov. 1:8; 2:1; 3:1; etc.) needed to be won for an
ideal that was not immediately self-evident or appeal-
ing to the prospective learner.

The wisdom teachers struggled with evangelistic
zeal to pull the "fool" away from the brink of death
to which the road of folly would lead him, and to
direct him towards life along the path of wisdom. The
latter was increasingly identified with *tôrāh*, until
the two became completely identified by the time of
Ben Sirach (1:26; 6:37 etc.). In this process they
developed an "anatomy of foolishness," distinguishing
between progressive degrees.[21] The "simple" (*pétî*;
e.g. Prov. 1:4, 22; 7:7), our "greenhorn" and the one
"without sense" (*hāsēr lēb*; literally: "empty of
heart"; e.g. Prov. 7:7f.) were still teachable. The
"fool" (*ĕvîl*; e.g. Prov. 11:29) and the "fool" (*kĕsîl*;
e.g. Prov. 10:18) represent the hardened fool who re-
sists teaching and creates trouble. Finally, the
"scoffer" or "scorner" (*lēs*; e.g. Prov. 29:8; 22:10,
3:34) and the "fool" (*nābāl*; Prov. and 1 Sam. 25:25;
Ps. 14:1) are the arrogant fools, who say in their
heart, "There is no God" (Ps. 14:1). We see here the
dedicated effort to achieve an educational ideal that

is religiously motivated and very sincere. It struggled against the odds of human sluggishness and sinfulness, but it undoubtedly achieved some of the finest fruits of education in ancient Israel (Ps. 1).

3. Finally, Israel did realize the limitations of a patriarchally oriented educational system in which learning was expected to flow from the old to the young. In part, this realization was based on observation and common sense:

> Better is a poor and wise youth
> than an old and foolish king,
> who will no longer take advice.
> (Eccles. 4:13)

The stance of Elihu in the Book of Job (32:6-10) must have been experienced from time to time. Here a young man politely awaited his turn to speak, but then he courageously contradicted the faltering attempts of Job's three friends to interpret Job's suffering. (Whether Elihu had something better to say is an open question.)

That the old is not always the better was also impressed on Israel by her history. Had it not been the Exodus-generation that had to die in the wilderness, while its children were allowed to enter the land? (Num. 14:29). It appears that the time of Jeremiah and Ezekiel, embracing the crisis of Jerusalem's destruction (578 B.C.), was especially cynical towards history:

> The father have eaten sour grapes,
> and the children's teeth are set on edge.
> (Jer. 31:29; Ez. 18:2cf. Lam 5:7)

The prophets counteracted this mood by affirming that each generation had its own chance:

> The son shall not suffer for the iniquity
> of the father,

nor the father suffer for the iniquity
   of the son.
(Ez. 18:20)

There was another limitation placed on the absolute primacy of the older generation, namely the
autonomy and the grace of God. Time and again, by
way of an unlikely choice, God chose the apparently
too young and inexperienced for his special tasks.
We think of the election of Joseph (in contrast to
his older brothers), Moses, Samuel (over against Eli),
David (as compared to his older brothers, and over
against Saul), and Jeremiah. In a sense, each new
generation is God's new opportunity.

Without abandoning her high view of the educational duties and capacities of the older generation,
ancient Israel acknowledged that God, in his sovereignty and grace, could override normal patterns and
choose the young and inexperienced for some of his
greatest tasks. As long as those who teach preserve
this insight, they retain a sense of wonder and mystery
toward their students who, in a sense, are their
inferiors, but who may far out-distance their teachers,
not only in human learning, but also in God's plans
for them.

III.

We must give brief consideration to the question
whether the educational patterns, as described, are
merely the timebound customs of a little people of
long ago, or whether they are inherently bound up
with and proper to that theology which they perpetuated then and which we Christians hold to be God's
word even for us today. It must be clear from the
beginning, that many of ancient Israel's ways of
teaching and learning belonged to a relatively unsophisticated, clan-centered, patriarchal agricultural
society and have lost much of their usefulness for
our cultural context. However, there are elements

in what have considered, I believe, that transcend
their own time and culture and are worth our ponder-
ing, if not our imitation.

    1. I believe that <u>the primacy of the parent-
child model in education transcends specific cultur-</u>   x
<u>al limitations</u>. As mentioned earlier, we find it even
among animals. Every society that considers the
family structure foundational will remind itself that
<u>educational efforts and institutions outside of the</u>
<u>family are merely extensions of parental right and</u>   x
<u>duty</u>. It has been a mark of absolutist and dictatorial
ideologies and systems that they attempt to wrest this
responsibility from the parents and transfer it to the
state.

    2. <u>All real knowledge and wisdom is handed from
the past to the future</u>. Educational experimentation
in our time with student-centered learning models, as
well as the high value placed by our society on recent
discoveries, may obscure this fact for us and suggest
to us that significant knowledge lies with the young
and "up-to-date," who have just left college or graduate school. This is deceptive, however. Even the
latest discovery rests on the foundations of the past,
and even the young teacher "speaks down" to the young
generation of learners from the platform of the older
generation, even <u>if he himself is a young person, for
he dispenses the knowledge of those who went before</u>.
That is why students will <u>consider even very young
teachers to belong to the older generation</u>. "This is
the first time I am discussing this problem with an
older person," a student told me once when I was a
very young college teacher. Upon checking the
records I found that he was only two years younger
than I. <u>Erik Erikson has gone so far as to make this
urge to care for the young by passing on one's values
the mark of proper identity development of the middle-
aged adult</u>; he calls it "generativity."[22] For the adult
generations to talk with young people who move towards
adulthood and to transmit knowledge and values in the
hope that these will be received, cherished, and de-

veloped--that is not authoritarian in an antiquated
and negative sense; it is healthy and responsibly
human. Where it does not happen, society is perverted
or sick. That such a flow of learning from the older
to the young should not be oppressive and authoritarian, but engage the mind, interest and collabora-
tion of the young, was known in ancient Israel already. The father's religious instruction was to be
elicited by the questions of the son whose mind had
been stimulated towards inner participation (Deut.
6:20-25; Ex. 12:24-27; Josh. 4:20-24).

3. As to method, much about education in the Old
Testament is accidental and time-bound. One aspect,
however, is inherent to biblical faith and should not
be lost in Christian education. It is the centrality
of story-telling in transmitting the faith. Deuteronomy 6:20-25 is once again a classical passage.
Religious questions are answered by telling the story
of God's great acts. The medium of the story is a
part of the message; it cannot be replaced adequately
by any other medium. God's revelation was experienced
by Israel as a series of incidents or stories that
flow together into a comprehensive story of God with
man. No audio-visuals, no charts, no deduction of
abstract doctrinal statements can or should replace
that method in the Christian Church.[23]

4. The wisdom emphasis of the Old Testament is
a further value to be retained. It is the empirical
search for God's orders in nature and in human life,
without the assumption that the insights gained are
valuable only if they can be demonstrated to be
consistently valid under controlled conditions. In
other words, and without any anti-scientific tendency whatsoever, the Church needs to affirm that
God gives us much significant access to an understanding of his world in ways more humble, but much
more comprehensive on the average, than our scientific efforts are likely to offer. We must not de-
valuate wisdom as a mode of understanding by limiting
significant insight to what is "scientific." The

attempt of the social sciences to pattern themselves
on the model of the natural sciences should not be
furthered by Christians nor carried over into theology and Christian education.

5. The preservation of learning and practice,
evident throughout the apprenticeship-centered education of ancient Israel, remains a desirable goal for
us. Certainly we must resist an impatient pragmatism
that presses for "practical applications" on every
step of the way. However, a search for knowledge that
is disinterested in its application to life and re-
fuses to take responsibility for the practical con-
sequences and applications of such knowledge is also
out of step with a biblical understanding of man as
the steward of God's world.

6. Finally, the Old Testament should remain our
model in its refusal to separate "religious education"
from "general education." The same parents who teach
the child to walk, to talk, to tend the sheep and to 𝗫
grind the flour are his teachers and models in matters of faith. While we cannot expect in a pluralistic society that communal institutions will perform
the functions of the Israelite village circle, we must
not allow our minds to separate any realm of knowledge
from any other. We must counteract the tendency of
the various disciplines to seek their own autonomy in
our time, by a comprehensive understanding of all
knowledge as rooted in the one God (Prov. 1:7).

IV.

Briefly, and by way of an epilogue, I wish to
point out certain developments in early Judaism that
may help us to connect the educational patterns of
ancient Israel with those of New Testament times.

The great educational institution of Judaism is
the synagogue. K. Hruby characterizes it as a place
of prayer and teaching.[24] Its precise time and mode
of origin are unknown, but it is widely accepted today

that it emerged either during or shortly after the
Babylonian Exile (598/587-539 B.C.), to meet the
religious needs of the Jewish community that had lost
its Temple.[25] The first trustworthy reference to a
synagogue comes from a relatively late Egyptian
source, however, namely an inscription from the time
of Ptolemy III Euergetes (246-221 B.C.).[26] By New
Testament times, synagogues were found in Palestine
and in many parts of the Roman Empire.

In spite of the meagre reports of its origins, we
can safely assume that the teaching functions of the
synagogue consisted, from the beginning, of the reading of the Scriptures, their translation into the
vernacular (Aramaic for Palestine; Greek for the
diaspora), and their exposition in a homily. Jesus'
participation in the synagogue proceedings of Nazareth
must have been quite typical (Lk. 4:16-30). It is
likely that men and women were segregated, both in the
Second Temple and in the synagogues. Women were not
obligated to attend synagogue services, but they could
do so and often did. They could also be called upon
to read the Torah. Some of them became learned in the
oral Rabbinic tradition.[27] On the whole, the teaching
function of the synagogue must have been akin to that
of a Protestant preaching service, with a somewhat
greater emphasis on the reading, as compared to the
preaching.

The emergence of the synagogue was paralleled, and
intertwined with, the development of a group of
specialists in the study of Scripture, the scribes.[28]
Their roots go back to two of the Old Testament's
educational models discussed earlier. First, we
observed that one branch of wisdom instruction at the
royal court was the training of young men as scribes,
in the secular sense, who would become the educated
civil servants. Secondly, we recall that the priests
were originally the custodians of tôrāh, i.e. religious instruction. As the Babylonian Exile removed
the need for a royal civil service, and as the new
emphasis on the study of Scripture required increasing

intellectual expertise, the learning of the wise and the educational duties of the priesthood must have merged to produce this new and important class of theologians and educators. Ezra is the scribe *par excellence*. Of priestly lineage, "he was a scribe skilled in the law of Moses" (Ezra 7:6). "For Ezra had set his heart to study the Law of the Lord, and to do it, and to teach his statutes and ordinances in Israel" (v. 10). From the emergence of the Pharisaic movement in the second century B.C., the scribes were associated closely with that movement, being its intellectual core. They became the lawyers and guardians of Scripture and produced the Rabbinic tradition, the intellectual-theological backbone of Judaism through the centuries.

While the synagogue was the central institution dispensing religious instruction in early Judaism, it was not a school in the customary sense of the word. There were various more or less organized efforts at group instruction in preexilic as well as postexilic times, carried on at the royal court, among the prophetic groups, and among the people generally by priests and Levites (Neh. 8:7-8).[29] Evidence for the existence of schools, however, comes only from rather late postexilic times. The first reference to a "school" (*bêt midrash*="house of seeking/study") is found in Sirach 51:23. The Talmud credits Simon ben Shetach, a contemporary of Alexander Jannaeus (103-76 B.C.) with the demand that children should be sent to school (*bêt-hassēpher*= "house of the Book"),[30] and Joshua ben Gimla, high priest between 63 and 65 A.D., is said to have decreed that every town should have a school for children from six or seven years up.[31]

It seems that public education was well estab-lished among Palestinian Judaism at least by the first century A.D. Whether the later Jewish educa-tional system of the Talmudic period and the Middle Ages, consisting of primary (*bêt sēpher*), secondary (*bêt midrash*), and higher schools (*jesîvāh*), can be read back into this time, is very questionable.[32] It

is interesting to observe, however, that these later
Jewish schools, though offering instruction in reading and writing, had as their aim the instruction in
Torah, rather than the pursuit of a general educational ideal.[33] Their curriculum consisted of reading from the Bible sentence by sentence, translating
it into Aramaic, and memorizing what was read. Next
came "Talmud," or oral interpretation, on the basis
of the written Mishnah. The highest level of Scriptural training, that of a rabbi, could be attained to
in the "Jeshivah," the school operated by a rabbi.[34]

In spite of this well-structured three-tiered educational system, Judaism, in the Talmudic period, and
even in the Middle Ages, considered the father to be
the person primarily responsible for the education of
his children, both in Torah and in a vocation. The
schools were established as a help to fathers who
were not in a position to carry out this educational
mandate.[35]

With this observation we recall the primary educational model with which we began our survey of
education in the Old Testament, the model of parent
and child. And the father's model as a teacher was
the great teacher of Israel, the Heavenly Father:

Behold, God is exalted in his power;
who is a teacher like him? (Job 36:22)[36]

FOOTNOTES

[1] Roland DeVaux states, "Writing was in common use at an early date." (*Ancient Israel*, New York: McGraw-Hill, 1965), vol. I, p. 49. Widespread literacy is also posited by J. Kaster, "Education, OT," *The Interpreter's Dictionary of the Bible*, Vol. E-J, p. 34. The evidence for such claims is rather limited, however, and we must assume that many in Israel were illiterate.

[2] On the tribal structure of Israel see DeVaux, *Ancient Israel*, vol. I, pp. 3-23; and Norman V. Gottwald, *The Tribes of Yahweh: A Sociology of the Religion of Liberated Israel, 1250-1050 B.C.E.* (Maryknoll, New York: Orbis Books, 1979), esp. pp. 237-341.

[3] Following Ludwig Koehler, *Hebrew Man*, trans. by P. R. Ackroyd (Nashville: Abingdon, 1957), pp. 74ff. See also my "Male and Female Roles in the Old Testament Outside of Genesis 1-3," *Still in the Image* (Newton, Kansas: Faith and Life Press, 1982), pp. 84-91.

[4] There are certain exceptions. Num. 1:3, 18; 26:2; 2 Chron. 25:5 set twenty as the age for military service. Ex. 20:14 gives the same age for taxation. On the basis of these, together with the judgment in Num. 14:29; 32:11 and the table of values in Lev. 27:1-8, Hans Walter Wolff concludes that "in general the 20-year-old counted as being completely responsible" (*Anthropology of the Old Testament*, trans. by M. Kohl, Philadelphia: Fortress, 1973, p. 121). A Levite began his service at the maturer age of 30 (Num. 4:23). See Wolff (*ibid.*, pp. 119-127) on the Israelite's stages of life, and Koehler (*Hebrew Man*, pp. 52-54) on the age of marriage.

[5] Although the statement that Ishmael was circumcised at the age of 13 (Gen. 17:22) has sometimes been taken to point to a special importance of that age for religious maturity, the Jewish custom of Bar-Mizvah, at age 13, is a later development and cannot be supported from the Old Testament.

[6] Koehler, *Hebrew Man*, pp. 86 ff.

[7] The nature of this mental activity is classically presented in Gerhard von Rad, *Old Testament Theology*, Vol. I, trans. by D. M. G. Stalker (New York: Harper, 1962), pp. 418 ff. For a full treatment of all aspects of wisdom in the Old Testament see von Rad, *Wisdom in Israel*, trans. by J. D. Martin (London: SCM Press, 1972).

[8] DeVaux, *Ancient Israel*, Vol. II, pp. 353-355: "The Priest as Teacher."

[9] See DeVaux, *Ancient Israel*, Vol. II, p. 354, and the standard Hebrew dictionaries.

[10] Hans-Joachim Kraus, *Theologie der Psalmen* (Neukirchen-Vluyn: Neukirchener Verlag, 1979), p. 113f.

[11] *Ibid.*, p. 113.

[12] See also DeVaux, *Ancient Israel*, vol. I, p. 49.

[13] Thus Ex. 28:3 speaks of all those "who have ability" (lit.: "who have a wise heart/mind," whom God has "endowed with an able mind" (lit. "a spirit of wisdom") to make Aaron's garments. Ex. 31:1ff. describes how God's Spirit has made Bezalel and other "able men" (lit.: "all who have a wise heart/mind") the ability to make the utensils for the Tabernacle (cf. also 35:10; 36:1, 2, 4, 8). Similarly, there is reference to all women who "had ability" (lit. "women who have a wise heart/mind") to spin; Ex. 35:25. Ezek. 27:8-9 refers to "skilled men" ("wise") outside of Israel who were pilots and those who could caulk the seams.

[14]DeVaux, *Ancient Israel*, vol. I, pp. 76-78.

[15]*Ibid.*, p. 77.

[16]On the subject of inter-generational relationships see Hans Walter Wolff, "Problems between the Generations in the Old Testament," *Essays in Old Testament Ethics*, edited by James L. Crenshaw and John T. Willis (Hyatt-Festschrift; New York: KTAV, 1974), pp. 77-95.

[17]Joachim Conrad, *Die junge Generation im Alten Testament* (Stuttgart: Calver Verlag, 1970).

[18]*Ibid.*, pp. 9-12.

[19]I am following Conrad in this threefold division in a general way, but the following sections are not a resume of Conrad's work. Cf. also my "Biblical Perspectives on Youth," *Still in the Image* (Newton, Kansas: Faith and Life Press, 1982, pp. 109-117.

[20]Wolff ("Problems," p. 84) treats this especially helpfully.

[21]Following John Paterson, *The Wisdom of Israel* (New York: Abingdon, 1961), pp. 64-68. Paterson may have classified too neatly; in many cases the terms for foolishness will have been used as synonyms. Nevertheless, the classification points to a mental effort on the part of the wise that is worth noting.

[22]Erik H. Erikson, *Identity: Youth and Crisis* (New York: W. W. Norton, 1968), p. 138f.

[23]Thus also Wolff, "Problems," p. 92.

[24]Kurt Hruby, *Die Synagoge: Geschichtliche Entwicklung einer Institution* (Zürich: Theologischer Verlag, 1971), p. 9 and n. 3.

[25]*Ibid.*, pp. 14-30; and H. H. Rowley, *Worship in Ancient Israel: Its Forms and Meaning* (London: S.P.C.K., 1967), pp. 213-245: "The Synagogue." Hruby explains how local worship services may well have been conducted at various places in Israel during the time of the Second Temple, or even earlier, and how such meetings may have developed into the synagogue (pp. 15ff.).

[26]Hruby, *Die Synagoge*, p. 19. This is a sober historical assessment. Rabbinic tradition, unhampered by questions of authenticity, traces the origin of the synagogue to Moses, or even beyond (*Ibid.*, pp. 27-30). We note parenthetically that "synagogue," like "church," refers both to the building and to the congregation gathering there.

[27]On the participation of women in the worship of the Temple and the synagogues see Hruby, *Die Synagoge*, pp. 50-55.

[28]A helpful account of the emergence of the scribes is given by Matthew Black, "Scribe," *The Interpreter's Dictionary of the Bible*, Vol. R-Z, pp. 246-248. Cf. also Kaster, "Education," p. 32.

[29]A good survey is offered by Kaster, "Education," pp. 30-33.

[30]Jerus. Talm. *Kethuboth* VIII, according to Donald E. Gowan, *Bridge Between the Testaments: A Reappraisal of Judaism from the Exile to the Birth of Christianity* (Second Edition, Revised; Pittsburgh, The Pickwick Press, 1980), p. 301. See also Kaster, "Education," p. 33.

[31]Bab. Talm. *Baba Bathra* 21a; *ibid.*

[32]Gowan, *Bridge*, p. 301.

[33]Johann Maier, *Geschichte der jüdischen Religion*
(Berlin/New York: Walter deGruyter, 1972), p. 111f.

[34]*Ibid.*

[35]*Ibid.*

[36]On this point see Kaster, "Education," p. 33.

RESPONSES TO THE PAPER

Eleanor Loewen: *I particularly liked the phrase, "conversation between generations." I think back to my growing-up situation after age nine when we moved to British Columbia. My grandparents moved there a year later and had a house on our yard. One of our unique opportunities as children was the "conversations between generations" and the consequent handing down of knowledge and wisdom from past to future. My grandfather was especially influential in this process, and I think it took some of the burden of responsibility for our spiritual nurture from my parents. I recall the evenings when the grandparents sat on the bench outside their house and we would go over to chat with them. That's where I learned to crochet; and while Grandma and I were crocheting, Grandpa would tell us stories about their life in Russia. It was also the time that we learned some special German songs and memorized Bible verses, which we seldom did in our own house. I think especially of the Psalms, such as Psalm 108 which was Grandpa's favorite. As I grew older, it was easier to take admonition from him than from my parents.*

Like the nurturing of faith in the Old Testament, it was a patriarchal setting. In the church we had a strong group of ministers, and the elder was the person who told us what was right and wrong. Sometimes this was very upsetting, like the incident when we were invited as a youth group to go roller skating in Vancouver and the elder came to our choir practice to give us some Old Testament basis as to why roller skating was wrong. I don't recall the passage, but none of us liked it.

Another aspect of our education was the German school on Saturday mornings, where we also got some of our religious training. After breakfast we headed out to the Mennonite Brethren church a mile and a half from our place. It wasn't until high school age that we became aware of the different Mennonite groupings. George Konrad [another Seminar participant representing the Mennonite Brethren Seminary in Fresno, California] and I went to the same high school, and we were just saying to each other that we didn't know until later that the MBs and GCs [General Conference Mennonites] were not supposed to get along. In that school we were just "Mennonites."

Waldemar spoke of the centrality of storytelling in Old Testament education, and I had to think of the Canadian young people who were part of the "great trek" last year. Five hundred young people boarded a train in British Columbia and traveled to Ontario with several days of study and fun together; but perhaps the most significant event was Peter Dyck telling them the story of how the Mennonites left Germany after World War II and went to Paraguay. These teen-agers were absolutely wrapped up in what he was saying, laughing at the right times and asking their parents afterward, "Why didn't you tell us these stories?" And they would say, "You didn't want to listen." On that "great trek," they were ready to listen; and I think that storytelling is becoming more important as a means of nurture for our young people.

Hearing Waldemar speak of the value of the wisdom emphasis in distinction to modern science, I had to think of an article I read recently about medical school qualifications and how extremely stringent they are and how undergraduates are saying that they don't have time to study the humanities because they have to be ready for those entrance tests. One wonders how persons trained in modern professional schools will find answers for the ethical and moral questions they are bound to encounter.

Marlene Kropf: *I am trying to put two things together from this paper. I enjoyed the description of the village circle as the people participated in the evening dialogue. I could almost hear and see it happening. The other thing that caught my attention was the storytelling associated with the festivals of the Jewish people. It was said that the festivals were great liturgical events, a time for retelling the stories of God's acts in Israel's history.*

The question I had as I read that was where in Mennonite settings are the stories of God's acts told and retold among us, just the stories themselves? There are many words spoken in Mennonite worship but not very much storytelling. One of the parts of my own journey right now is to attend a Catholic folk mass every few Sundays following our Mennonite worship service; and one of the things that has impressed me there is the retelling of the stories through the liturgy. The congregation participates in the reading of the biblical story, and I come away from those services with a sense of a drama that has just happened.

I've also become aware recently of some work that Jerome Berryman has done at the Institute of Religion at Texas Medical Center. He has an article, "Being in Parables with Children" [Religious Education 74:3, May-June 1979, pp. 271-85] and his point of view is that children as well as adults need to enter into the story for the experiences to become their own, and they don't need someone to tell them what the story means. They will live in the story, and the meanings will become apparent as those meanings intercept with their own lives and growth. Berryman has adopted a technique for retelling the parables of Jesus. He has made boxes, golden boxes, that contain the items needed for telling the parables. He thinks the parables are important because they are Jesus' own images of God. They are a direct link that we don't get anywhere else. In the hospital setting, adults or other children are trained to tell the parables; and they take the box down and find all the things they need to retell the story. If it's the story of the Good Shepherd, there are pieces of green, blue, and brown felt for the grass, the water, and the sheepfold. There are sheep figures and a good shepherd figure; and the teller simply tells the story as the child enters into the experience. Berryman may ask some questions that allow the child to probe into the story, but he does not offer an explanation. Instead, the parable is there, they've both entered into it, and the story comes alive for each of them at his or her own stage of development. They have found that the children in that hospital, many of whom are ill, of course, go back to the room where the parables are located and pick certain boxes off the shelf; and they can tell what kind of struggle and growth is happening for that child by the parable that is taken down.

I think that what we have not always understood and what the Jewish people did understand is that the story communicates its own meaning and at many levels at a time; and it carries within it the life that will grow for the people who participate in the story.

Pauline Kennel: I imagined that many of you have the same experience as I, having lived at one time as a child and youth in a rural farm community and being transported into a very different kind of community where we're trying to raise our own children, including the frustrations of trying somehow to incorporate some of the earlier values into the present urban situation.

Growing up in Freeport, Illinois, was a good experience in many ways. Our whole social life was tied to the church. Farmers helped each other, their families were together in each other's homes, and we were together at the church celebrating all kinds of events. When we came home from school, we participated with our parents in all the jobs that needed to be done on the farm. There was something very wholesome in sharing that total experience, in which well-founded values based on our faith in the Word were lived out. What a way to build self-esteem, knowing that you were an important part of that whole enterprise, not off on some fragmented life that our children in the city experience. Dad goes off to work in one place, mother goes off to work another place, children go off to school, they come home for a snack, and they go out with their friends, with little sharing time together.

On the farm our family had devotions every morning, starting the day together. We had an intentional sharing of faith, an intentional connecting of ourselves with the larger church as we prayed for people all around the world, for our mission projects, and for people in that local community who were in various kinds of trouble. I don't think there were many Sundays that we were not together for dinner with other families in the church, and those were fun times.

We talk about family clustering these days and how we can get together and wrestle with the problems of life and how we can pass on our biblical faith as we wrestle with those problems. As I have reflected on my own upbringing, it was those Sunday dinners and afternoons together where this happened. Of course, the women were working in the kitchen, and the men were talking together in the living room; but we kids could wander all over the house and were often listening to what was going on in both rooms. That's a rich tradition that has been terribly lost!

I had a teacher in that church who was like the Old Testament model of the master sharing life with the disciples. She often invited us junior high kids to her home, where we shared in some of the preparation that she needed to do, including the parties she planned for us. That woman affected so many young people in ways that carry on now that she's no longer living.

That congregation was not afraid to name the gifts of its young people. As a youth I was invited to be a team teacher for a Bible school along with a veteran teacher. Moreover, on Sunday nights we had the old [Christian Endeavor] topics, you know; and we teen-agers were asked to address the whole congregation. It blows my mind to recall that! In order to have enough to say that we could share with the whole congregation, we needed to study, to search the Word, to learn, and to grow. How could that but help call forth one's gifts and build one's self-image as a disciple?

And now it's the challenge of trying to nurture faith in a suburban Chicago church. Working with families is a tough task today--so many broken in spirit. Planning nurturing events for the whole congregation that might help us to know each other well enough to call forth the gifts of each. We try to do this as best we can, like the annual dinner we have where we share our roots, telling each other where we come from, showing artifacts we've inherited. There are some people who don't want to be a part of this; but there are always those families and single people and older couples who care enough about our children and youth and themselves to come together and to really make that a time of growing together.

Norman Kauffman: I want to express my deep appreciation for this paper. My first response is to say that this model from the Old Testament should lead to some kind of community restitution. Eleanor and Pauline reflected on their past and how their communities shaped their faith and lives. What has troubled me most in working with college age youth over the past dozen years has been their cynicism, resulting from a gap between what has been preached and taught and what they have experienced. I don't think I'm quibbling with the definition of religious education, but it has to be more than transmitting cognitive information. It must be a sharing and experiencing of a communal life or it ends in cynicism. We must find ways to translate the nurturing models in this document into the 1980s; and when people experience it, they will affirm it.

Leland Harder: Before we break up into our discussion groups, let's take a few minutes for plenary discussion at this point, directing our questions to Waldemar, with priority for questions of clarification but not excluding questions of interpretation and application.

PLENARY DISCUSSION

Linea Geiser: I was very aware of the patriarchal structure of the Old Testament community and want us to be aware that we no longer accept a patriarchal way of life, notwithstanding the fact that all of the presenters at this seminar-workshop are men! When we somehow identify the ancient village circle, which was primarily a gathering of men, with our circles where the dishes are hopefully done together and the women are equally participant, I don't want us to miss the discontinuities of this, while affirming the continuities.

Waldemar Janzen: I was giving the historical situation, and that's how it was. I taught a course in Old Testament anthropology several years ago and had a seminar on the role of women. It was a group presentation by two people, who came up with a dual position on the subject, i.e., one saw the Old Testament in its most positive light with respect to women, and the other saw it in its most negative light. In their research they had simply come to the conclusion that you can read the Old Testament in different ways. If you read a book like And Sarah Laughed, [The Status of Woman in the Old Testament, by John H. Otwell. Philadelphia: Westminster Press, 1977], you'll find an Old Testament that is as positive on the role of women as you find anywhere in the ancient world. And you'll find other literature and viewpoints that interpret the Old Testament in the opposite direction. So you can do both, and I think we shouldn't play games with it.

One important thing to note is that the Old Testament was not Judaism. Women did not go veiled. The Old Testament men and women talked freely with each other. The kinds of stories you've heard about Pharisees who would bump into a wall rather than look up into the face of a woman do not belong to the Old Testament period proper.

When we look back today from a modern period of world history when there is too much population rather than too little, we may think that women were in a second-class position or not valued fully when we read that the role of wife and mother was taken very seriously. But if you read Proverbs 31:10ff concerning the character of the ideal wife in relation to her husband, you get the feeling that she was highly respected and hardly a second-class citizen.

Ross Bender: Linea's comment reminds us of one of the difficult but neccessary tasks of this workshop, and that is to sift through not only this presentation but the others, recognizing the fundamental discontinuities between that world and ours, to see if there is anything that can be salvaged, or to say it more positively, to discern if there is anything that endures and to sort out the continuities from the rather large discontinuities--patriarchy versus an egalitarian structure of thought and living together, the emphasis on community versus today's emphasis on the individual person's growth and development, etc.,-- to see what there is that keys into our time and of use to us as educators. It will not be an easy task, but surely one of the more exciting tasks of this conference.

Anne Rupp: Waldemar's paper generalized from those times when the ancient community was relatively stable. Today we're living in a rather unstable society with all kinds of identity crises in Mennonite churches. I was wondering how Israel functioned in times of crisis, such as followed the Babylonian captivity. What happened to the "conversation between generations" in Babylonia?

Waldemar Janzen: We have so little tangible evidence, and so we have to extrapolate from what we do know from afterward. In Judaism following the Babylonian captivity, we get the preoccupation with geneologies. If you take the literary-critical approach and conclude that there was a priestly strand that was being written or coming into its final form in the time of the Babylonian captivity, it is that material that is particularly concerned with family trees and geneologies. The books of Chronicles start with some ten or eleven chapters of family trees. Extrapolating from what came afterward, we have to assume that the Babylonian captivity was a time of strengthening the clan and family structure; and I would suggest that this is a characteristic of hard times generally.

I came to Canada during the second world war, when the village structures in Russia had crumbled; and the same thing happened to us. Those who know about Mennonite life in the Soviet Union will know how they banded together by families; and it was also very evident among the refugees in Germany that families were torn apart and persons began to count as their family members only the nearest relatives. But as they found order out of chaos again, all kinds of lost cousins and uncles were found and the extended family bonds were strengthened.

By extrapolating from what came afterward, we have to assume that the Babylonian captivity was a time of strengthening the clan while nuclear family relationships were threatened, and I would suggest that this is a characteristic of hard times generally. I think the Mennonite tradition of finding common relatives is a part of our wandering history. If you do not belong to a place with a continuing history, at least you belong to a clan.

SMALL GROUP REPORTS

Dick Rempel for Group #1: We wrestled with the relative importance of history and continuity for a people, with particular reference to the place of history in Christian education. The six generalizations at the end of Waldemar's paper are assumptions to take into consideration, but we live in a pluralistic society which seemingly works full-force against the stream as it was found in the Old Testament. Our society works with experimentation for the future rather than with history from the past. Consequently, the younger generation will not listen to the "fathers." If we are to recover these six generalizations, we will need some radical rethinking and another twenty steps to get at them.

Lavon Welty for Group #2: Our group focused on two questions. First, toward what are we educated? And second, toward what are we educating? On the first question, we talked about the fact that the purpose of education in Old Testament times seemed to be wrapped up in who the people of God were, and we wondered whether their self-image tended toward provincialism or toward universality? On the second question, we examined the acceptance of parental and elder authority of that society with its traditional values and skills, and found ourselves asking whether or not we've gone too far in the direction of child-centered education as opposed to teacher-centered education.

Levi Miller for Group #3: We spent most of our time getting acquainted with one another, in relation to Ross Bender's categories of continuity and discontinuity between the Old Testament form of education and our own. We discovered that seven or eight of us came from the farm and rural community where we experienced many of the characteristics listed by Waldemar. Mention was made of the Paul-Timothy and the Life Planning programs in operation today and that they may be in continuity with Waldemar's discussion of the father's responsibility for the children's education. However, with several in our group, that flow was reversed. Instead of going from parent to child, which seemed normative there, it was from child to parent in their situations. It was pointed out that perhaps some of this is necessary discontinuity, which speaks also to the concern of women as well as children having more participation in the learning process. The question was raised as to where in Waldemar's description of Old Testament education as a "conversation between generations" was there sufficient place for a child to discover new things? Moreover, the paper assumed that the family unit is ideal; but the family units that many people find themselves in today are so fractured. How does the Old Testament speak to that situation?

James Schrag for Group #4: Our group report is a variation on everything that has been fed back so far. On the continuity-discontinuity question, the pessimistic comment was made, "The Old Testament community ideals are not recoverable. So what do we do with them? Are we taking our own sociological situations as seriously as we believe the Old Testament theologians took their own sociology seriously? We talked about the relationship between knowledge and wisdom and acknowledged that today there is a great confusion between those two values. The explosion of knowledge today does not necessarily mean a corresponding explosion of wisdom. We live in circumstances where young people are armed with more knowledge than their elders, but so often without the wisdom of experience and maturity. Do we even take the time in our technological society for wisdom to accrue? So what model of Christian education can best take this explosion of knowledge, but not necessarily wisdom, into account and deal with it?

Paul Unruh for Group #5: Not to repeat a lot of what's already been said, I'll focus on two or three small additions in question form. The question was raised about storytelling: do we still know how? There was some doubt expressed in our group about how many teachers and leaders today really know how to tell a story for educational purposes, not to mention an awareness of what the components of a good story really are. A second question had to do with the use of poetry, psalms, and symbols, in the educational process. The suggestion was made that recall and integration occurs more frequently in images than through the traditional ways of thinking. A third question had to do with the segregation in our Sunday schools on the basis of age and marital status, and how we can take a cue from the Old Testament in relation to the wholeness of their congregational setting and the fact that a given special need was often met by the special resource provided within the total community. In every age, persons with resources need to be able to give of themselves as much as others need access to those resources. Young people today need to hear and know that the welfare of older persons is dependent on opportunities given them to share what they've learned from life with the younger generation.

Helmut Harder for Group #6: Our group, also, just barely had time to get acquainted and to suggest a few areas needing further discussion. I'll mention these for the purpose of drawing out implications. The first one concerns the village gathering model, which intrigued us and which we felt must somehow be recovered. This was picked up to some extent by the respondents who reflected on their heritage. We were not sure whether we're irrevocably "over the hill" on that, or whether our mobile society can still recover that, but that question seemed important to us. The second question had to do with defining story--how broad was the definition that was being held out to us? Was it mainly or only verbal and personal, or can it be thought of more wholistically as involving the whole body in various other ways of telling stories? There was comment in our group that our personal experiences should be shared more frequently in educational process and in worship and liturgy. A third point had to do with the question of interrelating the various Old Testament models and whether or not the concept of community was the overarching umbrella that interrelated them, perhaps even occasionally overruling a model used by anyone in a deviant way?

Waldemar Janzen in response to the group reports: I think I hear two kinds of moods in these reports, and I find myself having neither. On the one hand, several groups sound as if they seized upon the Old Testament situation and asked with great immediacy, how can we apply this? When I deal with the Old Testament, I see the road from the Old Testament to today as a little longer than came through in some of the group reports. Sometimes when I study the Old Testament, I feel under some obligation but no great constraint to apply it, which is not simply to say, "Oh, the New Testament people and the systematic theologians will make it relevant for today, and I can just stay back there and make six points for what they're worth." But then the counter mood that I also felt was the preoccupation of other groups with the present. Their mood seems to be, "Today, things are different. What, if anything, can we do with the Old Testament today?" Actually, I think, the same sense of differences might apply to the New Testament; and here again my mood is different. I believe that what is today is not that firm and unchallengable, and I think that the Bible in both testaments has much more power to challenge our present life-styles than what I've heard come through so far.

NEW TESTAMENT AND EARLY CHURCH
PERSPECTIVES

George R. Brunk, III

Education[1] in the earliest Christian tradition
draws its significance from that tradition's essential characteristic as <u>a counter community confessing
an alternate value system to that of the larger society.</u> Crucial to the formation and survival of such a
community is the process by which it transmits its
faith values over against a social system which exer-
cises a molding force on its members. Every human
community is concerned with means for handing on its
tradition. A community within a community, i.e., a
counter community, must in addition face the competi-
tive formative influence of the larger community.
Such was the early church; such is the church in any
age when it maintains a believers' church stance in
the world.

The indispensable role of nurture within a community of faith is the fundamental link between the
Jewish educational practices and those of the early
church. That Jesus and the first Christian communities continue the practices of the Jewish tradition is simply a consequence of a shared vision of
faith--that God is calling a people into a pilgrimage
of saved and saving existence in history. In this
connection it is instructive to remember that education, which was always important in Israel, became
the object of even greater attention in the exilic
and post-exilic period when the people were a community within a community. Robert Ulrich observes
that "all the more for a people in the state of dis-
persion the uninterrupted transmission of its spirit-

al values and the acquisition of the language of the
criptures became a matter of self-preservation."[2]
his is the situation which characterizes the entire
ew Testament period for the Christian church.

The importance of the nurturing process is quite
elf-evident in the case of Jesus and the early church.
eferences and allusions to such a process proliferate
n the New Testament writings. Yet, at the same time,
ne is struck by the paucity of information which re-
eals the actual processes themselves, particularly in
he early church in comparison to the ministry of
esus.

In this study we will first survey the historical
ata that can be gleaned from canonical and non-ca-
onical sources. Then, in an attempt to probe more
eeply, we will search for literary clues in the New
estament literature to the practice of nurture and
ts underlying rationale.

. The History of Nurture in the New Testament Period

A. Jesus as Teacher of the Kingdom

Jesus was known to the Jewish crowds as a rabbi.
he immediate impression left by Jesus' activity
aused him to be associated with the Jewish rabbinic
eachers who more than any others were the educators
f the people. Both in manner of teaching and in
ontent of teaching a resemblance was present. Jesus
et forth the claims of God in the holy writings, he
aught in the synagogues, formed a circle of disciple
earners, debated with the scribes, was sought out to
ronounce on legal disputes, sat down to teach, and
sed the pedagogical techniques developed by the
abbis to aid the listener in memorization.[3]

This understanding of Jesus is not only the super-
icial reaction of the general populace; it is the
eliberate intention of the evangelists to portray
Jesus this way. The designation "teacher"

(*didaskalos*) is the most typical way others address him. The editorial descriptions of Jesus' activity prefer "teaching" over "preaching" as the inclusive term. Jesus also can describe himself as teacher (Matt. 10:24-25 and par.; 23:8; John 13:13-14).

While the teaching role of Jesus places him squarely in the rabbinic tradition, it is not adequate to understand him as teacher from that connection. The rabbis stand in the scribal tradition of post-exilic Judaism in which the interpretation of the Torah came to replace the prophetic and even the priestly role in transmitting faith and guiding the people in religious matters. Jesus as a teacher of Israel combines the role of wise man and prophet bringing both to a climactic point of greatness. This seems to be Jesus' own claim when, in response to the scribes and Pharisees, he stated that a "greater than Jonah is here" and "a greater than Solomon is here" (Matt. 12:38-42 and par.). We are clearly to understand this as a reference to Jesus who is the agent of the Kingdom of God in the time of fulfillment.

The implication of these observations is that Jesus unites many gifts and activities of the Old Testament tradition under the generic description of teacher. The idea of teaching as it appears in the Gospels is an inclusive one. It does not set a particular activity over against other types of activity. Rather it serves as an umbrella term to characterize the entirety of Jesus' work. We turn then to examine more closely the various aspects of Jesus' teaching role. In doing this, Jesus' message and his methods of teaching will also come into focus. The coherence of message and method will become evident.

Teacher as Interpreter. Jesus was most like a Jewish rabbi in his exposition of the will of God according to the scriptures. Jesus was rooted in the Old Testament and supported its authority. He was an interpreter of scripture. There is abundant evidence that he employed the hermeneutical principles of rabbis and sects of apocalyptic orientation. Yet Jesus was not received as a respected rabbi by the official guild. That rejection was determined in part by Jesus' claims to be more than a rabbi as will be shown in later paragraphs. In part, however, Jesus introduced certain interpretative principles that were novel and offensive. He called for a *radicalization of the will of God*. This was directly related to the demand for repentance in light of the arriving kingdom. It also was demonstrated in his critical attitude to the compromising tendencies of scribal interpretations. Jesus' approach to the Old Testament was to drive to the heart of the matter--the spirit of the text. This was the will of God which applied to the present time. Moreover, Jesus proposed the *restoration of the will of God*. He did not read the holy writings as if all were equidistant from the intention of God, as his teaching on divorce shows. Jesus searched out the primal will of God. This took the shape of a restorationist hermeneutic meaning that God's original, perfect will is discerned in the primordial events like the creation accounts.[4] This is the standard that is now operative.

Teacher as Example. Equally close to the rabbinic style is Jesus' formation of a group of learners, i.e., disciples, to be with him and to receive his instruction. The inner circle of twelve may well have been a theological statement symbolizing the new people of God. But the presence of a disciple band, not limited to the twelve, is to be related also to the practice of the itinerant teachers, the rabbis.

Among the Jews of Jesus' day the nurturing of children took place in the home[5] and in the formal schools of the *Bet Sefer* and the *Bet Talmud*. In the former the child learned to read the Torah; in the latter there was study and memorization of the oral law.[6] For the adults there were those settings in which the teaching took place--the *Bet Midrash*, the synagogue, and informal group meetings at meals or other occasions.[7] The principal *bet midrash* was connected with the Sanhedrin and its scribes. Many local "schools" of this type existed for the study of the Torah. These were centered around a particular personality--the rabbi--and were informal in structure and setting. These circles of teacher and disciples were characterized by a shared life. The student spent full time with the master assisting him in any way possible. The group shared a common purse. The learner participated in the works of charity in which the master engaged. This meant that learning took place in a context of formal teaching and life experiences. *Learning by example* was a particular feature of this educational process. Study took place in any public setting sometimes with the intent of allowing the general public to listen. In some instances the small group wandered from town to town. The local residents were expected to offer them hospitality. The usual method of oral teaching was predominantly that of question and answer.

The parallels in the Gospel accounts to most of these features are more than obvious. The main point of interest here is that the disciple-learner is formed by observing and doing the life pattern of the master as much as by the cognitive instruction. The language of "following" and "coming after" expresses this way of learning. As Grassi notes, "There are expressions which convey a very strong sense of imitation in the rabbinic language of discipleship."[8] With Jesus the command to follow appears to have the double connotation of (1) participation in the cause of the Master and (2) identification and practice of his way of life. The central statement of discipleship discloses both aspects: "If anyone is willing to come after me, let him deny himself, and take up his cross and follow me" (Mark 8:34). The aspiration of a pedagogy of teaching by example is classically stated by Jesus himself: "A disciple is not above his teacher, but every one when he is fully taught will be like his teacher" (Luke 6:40).

No doubt the ministry in deeds which are so prominent in Jesus' activity are to be seen, in part at
least, as a deliberate method of teaching. Admittedly,
in the case of Jesus the primary purpose of the miracu-
lous deeds of love is to demonstrate the presence of
the kingdom as present liberation from evil. This
gives them a uniqueness determined by the distinctive
message of Jesus. At the same time their function
within the communication strategy of Jesus is significant. The actions of Jesus display and demonstrate
the cause he espouses. The disciple both understands
the good news and knows what deeds are appropriate for
his own life.[9] This is profoundly important for kingdom learning. With the kingdom a new existence is
offered. But nothing can be learned which is totally
beyond present experience. A thing must be seen as
possible before it makes sense and can be appropriated.
The new creation reality of the Gospel must be seen if
it is to be learned.

Teacher as Revealer. Jesus was more than rabbi.
Even the crowds see something deeper in Jesus when
they acclaim him as a prophet. The same insight is
probably implied by the references which describe
Jesus as one who speaks with greater authority than
the scribes. This in turn can be related to the
manner in which Jesus speaks for God over against the
rabbinic tradition or for one part of the Old Testament over against another part--"you have heard. . .
but I say." The portrait of Jesus in the Gospel of
John is centered around the theme of Jesus as revealer of God. So in John 3, Nicodemus recognizes
Jesus as "a teacher come from God" immediately after
addressing him as rabbi. In Jesus' response he
characterizes himself as "he who descended from heaven,
the Son of Man." The Johannine prologue boldly as-
serts that he has made God known (1:18). But the
synoptic writers also know of this unique quality of
Jesus the teacher who speaks directly for God. First,
Jesus is the bearer of the Spirit who revives the prophetic gift in the last days--his baptism experience
has this as a primary emphasis. In Jesus, therefore,

the roles of teacher and prophet are combined. Second,
Jesus himself makes a direct claim to the role of
revealer: "All things have been delivered to me by
my Father;. . . no one knows the Father except the
Son and anyone to whom the Son chooses to reveal him"
(Matt. 11:27). It is the son himself who is teacher
from whom we must learn (11:29). Jesus as revealer-
teacher continues the role of the teaching prophet
while raising it to an absolute and incomparable level
by connecting it to his unique sonship.

Complementary to the role of revealer is the
central, distinctive message which Jesus proclaims--
"the time is fulfilled, and the kingdom of God is at
hand; repent, and believe the gospel" (Mark 1:15).
Such a message is a disclosure, a revelation. It
lays a claim of God before the listener and its authority rests essentially in the speaker. This is
truth in the prophetic mode and the form of communication is announcement. Therefore the language of
preaching (*keryssein*) in the Gospel accounts is appropriate. At the same time it is done by the
teacher--but as revealer. Teaching the kingdom, of
necessity, partakes of proclamation because it informs
the listener that a new situation, external to him,
has come into being. The consequent call to repentance does not focus on moral regeneration solely or
even primarily. The accent falls on the reorienta-
tion of one's whole life around the changed situation
determined by the divine action in history. The rule
of God, i.e. the kingdom, is presently at work in and
through Jesus as its agent. The kingdom retains its
future dimension, for the completion of the divine
action is still awaited. However, the kingdom is present to the extent that it modifies, qualitatively,
the present situation of all persons.[10]

The characteristic medium by which Jesus communicates the kingdom announcement is the saying or the
pronouncement story in which a saying is the main
point. These short terse formulations were typical
of the teaching sages in Judaism and were preferred

because of the ease with which they could be remembered and handed on. For Jesus they open a new
world of understanding by proclaiming a new reality or
new demand of God. The parables and stories to be
discussed below share this characteristic. No example
of this quality of Jesus' sayings is clearer than the
beatitudes which proclaim a reversal of value system
in life and bring to realization a new condition in
the hearer by the pronouncement of blessing as a present fact.

In the case of teacher as revealer we move into a
special meaning of teaching and nurture. This is more
than the Socratic method because the hearer does not
possess the content of these learnings in a latent
fashion. While the distinctiveness of Jesus' person
sets this role apart from every subsequent Christian
teacher, every teacher who stands in this tradition
must adopt a style of teaching that does justice to
the revelatory character of the content and its consequent mode of appropriation.

Teacher as Re-visionist. It is evident that,
given the sort of message Jesus brings, a major educational task is required to convey the message.
Jesus does not merely transmit a religious tradition
or reinforce the current situation. He is obliged to
overthrow the present; he is a change agent. The purpose of his teaching is to subvert the old and to
construct a new--a reconstruction of the kingdom of
God.

By means of the parable teaching especially, Jesus
helps the listener to envision a new condition of
life. The parable pictures a particular state of
affairs. The hearer is able to see life in a new way--
the way of the kingdom. The teacher, in this sense,
is a re-visionist for through the formulation and re-
citation of the parable the listener is provoked into
a new vision of life as God would have it. "Parables
stir the imagination and stimulate personal involvement and search."[11] In this way the teacher becomes a
shaper of human life and destiny.

Parables have been fittingly defined as "meta-phorical stories,"[12] i.e., a narrative of an event or typical experience of life that illuminates, by way of analogy, the religious dynamics of life. As such they combine the power of the story to evoke interest and involvement with the genius of metaphor to create a picture of life from a new perspective. The new research on parables emphasizes their irreplaceable and irreducible character. They carry truth in a unique form. In the words of Ezra Pound, parable communicates by image rather than by idea. To pre-serve the original force, the image has to be re-tained. Parable can only be retold if its full effect is to be repeated. It is understandable that the early church used the parable material in its teaching ministry preserving it both in oral tradition and in the gospel writing. This is proven already by the fact that at least thirty-five percent of the recorded teaching of Jesus is made up of parables.[13]

Jesus' uniqueness as a person as well as in terms of his message is indicated by the parables he told. Parables are found in the rabbinic material but not predominantly as in Jesus' teaching. On the other hand, the early church did not create parables. In-stead they remembered and retold Jesus' parables. Yet, while the early Christians did not create metaphorical stories, they did continue the story-telling practice of Jesus. They could only depend on the new kingdom metaphor of Jesus by repeating the sayings and stories of Jesus, but they created their own historical narrative[14] of Jesus' life and work. This latter process led ultimately to the composition of our present four Gospels which incorporate the original teaching of Jesus *and* the church's story about Jesus.

B. Message and Method in Jesus' Teaching:
    Summary Evaluation

We have developed a profile of Jesus as teacher around the concept of interpreter, example, revealer, re-visionist. In each use a particular method was associated with the characterization. This has been done in order to bring out the unity of method and message. Jesus shows himself as a master teacher in the sense of using methods which are effective as means of communication. But more significant is the complementarity of method to the particular message Jesus offers. The methods Jesus adopts enhance the message itself. The connection of a method with a particular role should not be pressed. The revelation of God's will and purpose in the kingdom teaching prevades the material. The use of imaginative language characteristic of the parables/stories typifies Jesus' sayings as well.[15] The chief point is that message and method form an inseparable reality in assessing Jesus as a teacher.

The survey of Jesus as a teacher has suggested that the sharp distinction of preaching and teaching (*kerygma* and *didache*) does not hold in the case of Jesus. At least the Gospel writers do not see significance in the distinction. As example one can take Mark 1:21 and 39. In the first reference Jesus teaches in the synagogue at Capernaum. The second reference is a summary statement speaking of Jesus' preaching in the synagogues of all Galilee. The first is a specific instance of the second. The parallel to Mark 1:39 in Matthew 4:23 reads, "And he went about all Galilee, teaching in the synagogues and preaching the Gospel of the Kingdom." Here the synagogue activity is described as teaching, but the preaching of the gospel of the kingdom appears to be the same activity as the teaching. Fitzmyer observes of teaching in the Gospels--"It should not in the long run be made to imply an activity of Jesus that is different from his preaching."[16]

There are certainly grounds for seeing in Jesus' public ministry the distinction which is made today between monological and dialogical modes of communication. Modern usage tends to use the preaching/ teaching distinction to correspond to these respective modes. This distinction as noted, is not made in the Gospels. Jesus did use both the one-way and two-way forms of communication according to the situation and the content.

Along similar lines one can ask how Jesus' teaching fits the distinction between content-centered and student-centered methods. In Jesus these two aspects appear to be held together in a sensitive balance. It was pointed out that the inherent nature of the kingdom message causes a content-centered component to appear in his teaching. At the same time Jesus is a master of the socratic method of question-answer which is intended to obligate the hearer to interaction, response and commitment. On occasion the two approaches are closely combined as when a parable is followed by a question. So at the end of the story of the Good Samaritan Jesus asks the lawyer to confess which person in the account was neighbor to the victim of robbery (Luke 10:36 and cf. Luke 7:42).

Furthermore, what about the distinction between an evangelistic proclamation that calls to faith and teaching for nurture? Is this present in Jesus? Again we have to observe that the preaching/teaching word usage does not carry this distinction in the Gospels. There is evidence, however, of a difference in the teaching content in relation to whether the audience is the disciple circle or the larger crowds. The Gospels speak of Jesus withdrawing from the crowd in order to instruct his disciples. According to Matthew the Sermon on the Mount was delivered to the disciple band. Its content is clearly intended for the edification of the committed disciple. Mark and Matthew in their special ways speak of the special assistance Jesus gives the disciples in understanding the "secrets" of the kingdom. Luke presents a travel narrative of Jesus' journey from Galilee to Jerusalem during which special attention is given to teaching for the disciples. John's Gospel dedicates an entire section to "nurture" of the disciples in the upper room discourses (chapters 13-17).[17] We are justified then in noting a movement from the proclamation of a basic call to belief (*kerygma*) to developed teaching regarding the life of the follower (*didache*). The point of demarcation between the two cannot be identified. Moreover, in the light of current misunderstandings, we must stress that the central theme of discipleship in Jesus' teaching does not correspond to nurture (*didache*). "To follow Jesus" describes both initiatory and developmental stages, relational as well as vocational dimensions of the believer's experience. Perhaps the most significant point is to note the blurring of the distinction of *kerygma* and *didache* in the evangelism (call to belief) of Jesus. As noted already Matthew has Jesus directing the Sermon on the Mount to disciples. However, at the end of the sermon we are told of the reaction of the crowds who overhear the sermon. Luke's parallel Sermon on the Plain is even more explicit about the overlap and interplay of the audience. Disciples and crowds are present, but when Jesus speaks he looks toward his disciples. The sermon closes with the note that Jesus had spoken in the hearing of all the people. The clear implication of this situation is that the "didache" of the sermon is not without "kerygmatic," i.e., evangelistic, relevance. We could say that the *didache* is part of the *kerygma*.18

C. The Teaching Ministry in the Early Church

Teaching is a prominent gift and role in the early communities whose life is reflected in the canonical writings. The teaching function appears immediately in the post-resurrection situation. Jesus himself continues the teaching he had began in his earthly lifetime (Acts 1:1, 3). As soon as the early circle of believers come together in post-Pentecost Jerusalem, their life is marked, among other things, by the teaching ministry of the apostles. From this point on teaching is a dimension of all Christian communities. The importance of the teacher in the Jewish Christian groups is made clear in James. "Teacher" is the self-description of the author ("we who teach," 3:1) and

the teaching role is to be taken with utmost serious-
ness because of the greater accountability attached to
it (3:1). In the mixed Jewish and Hellenist congregation at Antioch prophets and teachers were active
(Acts 13:1). Throughout the writings of the Apostle
Paul teaching is mentioned regularly as part of the
gifts which are exercised in the church (Romans 12:7;
1 Corinthians 12:28; Ephesians 4:11).

In the early church there appears a greater
tendency to differentiate the teaching role from
other modes of communicating the faith. Wegenast
seems to be correct in asserting that teaching in the
Gospels refers to Jesus' proclamation of his essential
kingdom message while in the later epistles it denotes
the instruction in the content and doctrine of
Christian faith.[19] The teacher is identified in con-
tradistinction to prophets, evangelists, apostles,
and pastors. At the same time these were not roles
that could not be filled by the same person. The
first teaching was done by the apostles (Acts 2:42)
and they presumably always had a teaching role in
their position of witnesses to the life of Jesus. In
the reference above to prophets and teachers in
Antioch, the three persons so described were apparently characterized by both functions. Teaching is
shared by all ministries and even by the entire
church.[20] The latter is seen clearly in Colossians
3:16 and Hebrews 5:12.

According to Groome the teachers in the early communities shared with other ministries the communication of the Word. They differed in that they "attend
deliberately to the process by which people came to
incarnate the Word in their everyday existence."[21]
In contrast to the evangelist who announced the basic
message, the *kerygma*, the teacher had "the task of
formation, of sponsoring people to embody the Word in
their everyday lives."[22]

The implication is that *kerygma* and *didache* are more distinguishable in the early church than in Jesus. This is probably the case and may be due to the fact that (1) the several roles tended to concentrate on separate individuals given differing natural or spiritual gifts and (2) in the continuing life of the church the wider gap between the new believer and the matured member created a greater perceived and real difference in teaching content. In fact, on the latter point the reluctance to mature in the faith became a problem threatening the strength of belief. This led the writer of Hebrews to call his readers to move beyond the elementary teachings to the solid food of maturity (Hebrews 6:1).

However, in this case as in the case of Jesus' ministry (see above) it is highly important to place a limitation on the difference of proclamation and teaching/nurture. The epistolary literature which reflects the teaching and nurture stage in particular displays a consistent inclination to reach back into the foundational events of the gospel for clues to the current ethical issues in the community. The clearest evidence of this procedure is the use of the early hymnic statements of faith embedded in the epistles to ground the practical exhortations for Christian living. In light of the tendencies to fixation of doctrinal and moral material in the Pastorals, it is all the more significant that the "faithful sayings," which express basic elements of belief, are cited to undergird the practical admonitions. Since both the confessional hymns and the faithful sayings are predominantly Christological in content, we can point to the presence of a "Christological reasoning" pattern that is pervasive.[23] This bridging of *kerygma* and *didache* is of fundamental importance for Christian self-understanding. Any sharp distinction between the two risks an isolation of ethics from their theological grounding in the new creation work of the Spirit and therefore exposes ethics to legalism (cf. Galatians 3:1-5).[24]

What was the method of this early teaching/nurtur-
ing ministry? Rengstorf is probably correct in describing the content as consisting primarily in exegesis of (Old Testament) scripture and in exhortation.[25]
The teacher is no doubt to be connected especially
with the transmission of tradition. In this way the
role would approximate that of the Jewish rabbis.[26]
The technical language of Jewish tradition--receive/
hand on--is present in the church's literature (1
Corinthians 11:23; 15:1-3). The content of the
Christian tradition centered around the scriptural
tradition (the Old Testament) and the new Christian
tradition composed of three types: the *kerygmatic*
tradition, the church tradition, and the ethical
tradition.[27]

The early Christians developed a form of Old
Testament interpretation that took its forms from the
practices of Judaism and its presuppositions and from the
actual practice of Jesus.[28] The teachers appear to
be the special practitioners of instruction, transmitting this form of scriptural interpretation. In
summary, this use of the scripture can be described
as the correlation of the divine purposes revealed in
the Jewish scriptures with the new revelation of God
in the events centered around and precipitated by
Jesus of Nazareth. While the Old Testament could be
used for moral guidance, the principle usage was in
the *pesher* mode[29] that made the current events of
God's action the hermeneutical key to the scripture
and the scripture as clarification and guarantee of
the present acts as indeed the acts of the God of
Israel. This was carried out in a reliance on the
prophetic gift of pneumatic understanding given by
the Spirit of God.

The *kerygmatic* tradition was composed of the
earliest confessions of faith centered in the work of
God in Christ in his death, resurrection, and as-
cension. Probably the early narratives of the passion
and of the resurrection appearances also were first
used in this way. Although the *kerygmatic* tradition

vas used primarily in evangelistic and apologetic-
proclamation, the teachers also would appeal to the
foundational material (as shown above).

The church tradition refers to the accumulating
experience of the early communities and had to do with
matters of church order and morality. The epistles
contain evidence of the appeal to common practice
among Christians for exhorting others to follow certain forms of behavior. The early teacher quite certainly became a communicator of the convictions
developed in the discernment and testing process of
the many single communities of faith. The introduction to Paul's epistles disclose an interest in the
exchange of stories among the congregations. The
book of Acts represents the final point of arrival of
this practice--a composite picture of the story of
the primitive church that has the purpose of con-
firming the faith of later generations of believers
(Luke 1:1-4, especially verse 4).

The ethical tradition was the primary concern of
the early teacher. Where this tradition is something
other than the church tradition, its focus is the
Jesus tradition, i.e., the remembered material from
Jesus' life and teaching.[30] The content of this
tradition was the sayings and narratives originating
with Jesus. We noted that the evangelistic preaching
had interest in certain limited aspects of this tradition, especially the passion and resurrection accounts. But it seems likely that the teaching minis-
ry is where the bulk of the Jesus tradition was kept
live and passed on. Current scholarship has found
evidence for collections of miracle stories and chains
of thematically related sayings which antedated the
gospel narratives. The probable setting for these
collected materials was the teaching work in the
churches. They were intended for ready memorization
and recollection.

A more obscure aspect of the transmitting of the
Jesus tradition has to do with the more extended

stories of Jesus himself such as the Prodigal Son or the stories about Jesus (infancy narratives or the Emmaus account of the resurrection). Some have supposed, with plausibility, that a story-telling role was filled by certain persons in the communities. In this way the stories of Jesus were remembered and recounted, and the stories about him were developed and refined. All we can say with reasonable certainty is that story telling was part of the nurturing activity that went on among the Christians. This is the only way to explain the presence of these stories in our Gospels

The use of the Jesus traditions gave to the teaching of the early church a central focus and objective which can be described as the formation of Christ in the believer, to use a Pauline expression (Galatians 4:19; Ephesians 4:11-13, esp. v. 13). The possibility of contemplating the glory of God in the face of Jesus and of being transformed into his likeness (2 Corinthians 3:18-4:6) must ultimately be connected with one's exposure to the story of Jesus of Nazareth. This must apparently be affirmed in spite of the celebrated difficulty in documenting the relationship between the teaching approach of the epistles and the large body of tradition deposited in the Gospels. The most plausible theological rationale for these documents which resulted from the preservation of the Jesus tradition, i.e., our four Gospels, is the need felt by the church in its nurturing ministry to hold the mirror of Jesus' whole life before the believer in order that s/he might "be conformed to the image of God's Son" (Romans 8:29).

II. *The Practice of Nurture according to the New Testament Writings*[31]

There is another line of investigation to be pursued in order to see more deeply into the educational process in the early communities. This has to do with a more in-depth reading of portions of the New Testament documents which disclose through content or form the manner in which the nurturing process was conceptualized and practiced. This discussion will be marked by brevity and suggestiveness due to the limitations of this paper. Several books or portions will be used to illustrate different aspects of nurture or different approaches to it.

A. Nurture in the Counter-Community: 1 Peter

As noted in the introduction of this study the concept of education is profoundly influenced by the social matrix in which it takes place. Where a stable, monolithic society is the ideal, socialization of the individual for conformity to society will be the objective of the education. In the case of the counter-community, the goal of education will be a mixture of socialization into the community but critical discontinuity and nonconformity in relation to the larger society (and to the community itself in its tendency to unfaithfulness).

The epistle of 1 Peter is the clearest picture of the church as a counter-community that we have in the New Testament. "This is the only New Testament writing which systematically and thematically has addressed the issue of Christian alien residence within the structures of society."[32] According to John Elliott in a recent sociological interpretation of 1 Peter, this Christian fellowship developed an ideology based on the Christian community as an alternative socio-religious structure, a home for the homeless in the midst of an alien society. "The idea of the community as the *oikos tou theou* [household of

God] functioned as the chief integrative concept of
1 Peter."[33]

One searches in vain for any particulars regarding
the nurturing activities of this community. A general
picture emerges, however, that is consistent with the
rest of the New Testament. The word of God, both in
the form of preaching and Old Testament scripture, is
the element of nourishment (1:23-2:3; 3:5, 6, 10-12).
The community is made up of members who are each gifted
to be a medium of God's gracious action to benefit the
growth of the community by word or deed (4:10, 11).
Elders especially carry out ministries of teaching and
example setting (5:1-5). The emphasis in evangelism
and nurture is on a learn-by-example principle (2:12;
3:1, 16 and 5:3, 5). We are certainly correct in
seeing the epistle itself as an illustration of the
teaching style among the elders since the writer is
himself an elder (5:1). This style can be characterized as an appeal to present action based on Old
Testament and Jesus examples, the essential spirit of
previous Christian experience, and an eschatological
outlook that reaches beyond the present decadence
toward future salvation.

These points are illuminating but what is of
special force from the epistle is the definition of
the task of nurture implicit in the description of
the community's posture in society. What is that posture? Elliott suggests four features: a sense of
distinctiveness, readiness to suffer, a radical sense
of community, an accentuation of the familial and
household character of the community.[34] The picture
that emerges is that of ecclesiastical solidarity combined with social engagement. The church possesses a
keen self-identity and, at the same time, is intensely
involved in the structures of the larger society.

This Christian group has taken to itself the
status of family and makes its claim against the kinship grouping of society as well as ethnic or political groupings.[35] This self-understanding as family

meant that the relationship of the believing community to the biological family is an ambivalent one--a love-hate relationship. The faith community claims priority over the biological by constituting itself over against the other. Yet by taking for itself the form and function of family, the faith community acknowledges the validity and enduring value of the family and seeks its cooperation in building the household of God in the midst of history.

What then is the character of nurture implied by this particular kind of community? In summary form--it is both world-affirming and world-denying, i.e., it prepares the believer to know the world in a critical fashion by applying the criterion of righteousness and holiness to society (3:14-16; 4:1-5). It is past-oriented in the history of God's wonderful deeds (2:9) and future-, change-oriented toward the new world of hope (1:3, 13; 3:9). It is individual-oriented and community-oriented because it prepares each believer to participate in the construction of a "spiritual house and a holy priesthood" (2:5). With this we turn to another text for additional insight to see how this edifying took place in a Pauline church.

B. Nurture in the Familial Community: Colossians

The imagery of the Christian community as a house-hold is not unique to 1 Peter. Paul also uses family metaphors for describing the church. In fact, according to R. P. Martin the image of family of God is the foundational metaphor of the New Testament view of the church, having a priority over the other principle images of temple and body.[36] These latter images speak to the functions of worship and service respectively, but the family image speaks to the foundational self-identity which makes the functions possible.

The family imagery underlies the description of Colossians 3:16 which, for all its brevity, is the most specific statement of how the nurturing process was expected to take place. The description is built

around the picture of the word of Christ making its
home (*oikeó*) with the household of faith. The word of
Christ has its productive effect through the teaching,
admonishing and singing of the members in the household.

Before commenting further on the implications of
this picture we can note from the larger context in
the Colossian letter the explicit goal of Christian
teachings--the presentation of "every man mature in
Christ" (1:28). This is reflected throughout the
epistle and specifically in the realization of the
creator's image (3:10). That image is mediated in
Christ who is the image of God (1:15; 2:9) and the
totality of reality for the body of believers (3:11,
15). The goal is the embodiment of a Christ-likeness
in the individual and collective life of believers.
The collective aspect, in fact, predominates in the
positive picture of the new nature--forgive each other,
forbear with one another, love one another (3:12-15).

This new community of Christ is nurtured into this
new existence by a divine empowering, taking the form
of the peace of Christ which must be allowed to hold
sway in its midst. Along with that expressly divine action is another that touches the educational
task of the community--freeing the word of Christ for
productive action through the specific activities of
teaching and admonition, on one hand, and singing,
on the other.

Several observations must suffice to define the
form of nurture here envisioned:

1. The specific content which constitutes the
substance of nurture is *the word of Christ*. This is
the message that carries the richness of God's will
made known in Christ. It is the person-related
knowledge of Christ that becomes communicable in the
language of human intercourse. This is call to a
Christ-centered agenda for nurture that corresponds to
the nature of this new community for whom "Christ is

all, and in all" (3:11). God works through the forms
of human communication (*logoi*) in producing the effect
of newness. Of interest is the image of the word
which resides or dwells in the midst of the community.
This is no transient encounter; it is a life together
in the living presence of the message. The word of
nurture becomes in every sense "a household word."[37]

2. The special contribution of this text to our
investigation is the explicit reference to a methodology of nurture. The word of Christ, which is in itself a means of divine operating, chooses the human
modalities[38] of teaching/admonishing and singing.
What is striking here is that, in contrast to the
common emphasis in the synagogue and in the modern
church on nurture as teaching, the nurture in this
congregation involves the worship celebration (singing). Indeed the following verse (17) which speaks of
"everything you do, in word or deed" implies that
everything in the community's life is curriculum for
nurture in Christ. Even the teaching is not mere
instruction but an active involvement in the personal,
spiritual welfare of others in the ministry of admonition.[39] The nurture here promoted combines formal instructional activities with person-changing concern (admonition) and celebrative participation which
allows the learner to appropriate and internalize the
truth by self-expression.[40]

3. The type of nurture spoken of is shared by the
entire group of believers. This is obviously true of
the "singing" but is stated clearly with the teaching
and admonishing by the expression "one another." This
does not negate the particular role of teacher. Paul
uses the same verbs of teaching and admonishing to
describe his ministry (1:28). That Paul held firmly
to a nurturing role for the entire community is even
more clearly asserted in Romans 15:14: "I myself am
satisfied. . . that you yourselves are . . . able to
instruct (*didaskein*) one another."

4. The text reveals a concern for what might be called the atmosphere of nurture. The context is marked by repeated exhortations to thanksgiving. The giving of thanks is part of the picture of worship that is an aspect of the community's growth into Christ. Thanksgiving denotes an attitudinal posture ("thankfulness in your hearts") of openness and responsiveness to God in his acts of grace. That the attitudinal dimension is pertinent to the learning process seems clearly implied. The relationship is not explained although the connection is not difficult to fill in.[41]

In conclusion, the Colossian letter proposes the household or family model for nurture. In this model relational learning rather than information flow is the aim. The entire life of the family is a source, means or support in the formation of the family members. One of those interacting "members" in the household is the word of Christ. That in particular determines the Christian household.

C. Nurture in the Remembering Community: Matthew and Luke

The Gospels are both the literary deposit of the teaching of Jesus of Nazareth and, simultaneously, the deposit of the earliest church's teaching ministry which had utilized the Jesus traditions. We traced the main lines of this development at the close of Part I, noting that the Gospels as we have them represent the end result of the use of materials from Jesus' life in the teaching work of the early church. In what follows we look briefly at the way two of the Gospels reflect particular approaches to the nurture process as revealed in the literary form and the historical allusions.

1. Matthew--Educator of God's People

It is the apt description of P. Bonnard that Matthew is "an educator of Christian people."[42] Whether

he was conscious of the fact or not, Matthew fills the
role of an understanding disciple whom Jesus describes
as a "scribe who has been trained for the kingdom of
heaven [who] is like a householder who brings out of
his treasure what is new and what is old" (Matt. 13:
52). The way in which the Gospel of Matthew uses both
the Old Testament *and* the words of Jesus as a source
of old and ever new shows that the evangelist attempts
to serve as a faithful scribe.[43] Yet here again the
teaching mission is shared by the entire body of
believers because the Lord's commission to the church
is to "make disciples of all nations . . . teaching
them to observe all that I have commanded you."

Standing as it does in the Jewish tradition, the
community of Matthew emphasizes the teaching function
by highlighting the role of Jesus as teacher and by
portraying the Christian congregation much like a
Jewish synagogue. Martin characterizes the Matthean
view of the church as a "Christianized *beth ha-midrash*,
a house of instruction in which Jesus is the great
teacher (11:28-30; 23:8-10), and in which faith and
knowledge go hand in hand."[44]

Consistent with this view of the church is the
way the material from Jesus is given a didactic turn
in order to bring out the implications of Jesus'
words and deeds for Christian living. In Matthew
the disciples do not reflect the faith-unbelief dynamics of Mark's Gospel. They are "model believers who
advance in the school of Christ."[45] The same is true
of Luke's Gospel. In other words the gospel account
becomes a "written model" of Christian behavior.
Learning by model and learning by word come together.
The clearest clue to this role of the disciples is
Matthew's unique designation of them as persons of
little faith. Believers are seen as persons whose faith
must be in constant development because even "model
disciples" must learn to acknowledge their lack of
faith even while standing under the call to be perfect
as the Father is perfect (5:48). One understands then

χ why nurture is a necessity in the community--life is an
✓ unending growth toward the full will of God.

Recent study has shown also that the very literary
shape given to the gospel tradition reflects Matthew's
didactic interests. We can use Bonnard's summary of
Matthew's pedagogy to illustrate the point.[46] *First,
his style was scholastic.* The miracle stories such as
the stilling of the storm or the feeding of the multi-
tudes are told in unadorned, concise style (compared
to Mark) but use the catchwords of exhortation and
devices typical of the time to assist in memorization.[47] The stories do not speak only of Jesus and
the kingdom presence but call the believer to a faith
for true discipleship. *Second, Matthew's style is
practical.* The accent is on concrete action. (See
especially the conclusion of the Sermon on the Mount,
7:15-27.) There is heavy use of the verb *thelo* meaning to desire or wish which underscores the voluntaris-
tic or ethical concern of the material. *Third, the
style is eschatological.* It is the essence of biblical eschatology to appeal for ethical response in the
present time. But Matthew gives a particular emphasis
on the moral incentive of the Last Judgment. A comparison of the apocalyptic discourses of the synoptics
easily shows that all three have Jesus note the appeal for moral readiness, but that Matthew, by adding
parable material, has accentuated the point.

2.   Luke--Storyteller for God's People

In a manner parallel to Matthew, Luke has utilized
the Jesus traditions for purposes of nurturing the
people of God. It is readily acknowledged that the
Lucan writing reflects a pastoral concern for the
spirituality and morality of his readers. Yet Luke
is writing for the Greek cultural setting in contrast to the marked Jewish setting of Matthew. Their
similarities and differences are instructive in terms
of the constants and variables in early church nurture.

Luke gives major attention to life in the Holy
Spirit and the experience of prayer. He is careful
to point out the manner in which the early communities
in Acts are committed to put into effect the jubilee
vision of Jesus (proclaimed in the programmatic sermon at Nazareth) by the shared life of spiritual and
material resources. The suffering of Jesus is used as
a means to arm believers with the same mind, to the
point of obscuring but not denying the atoning significance of the cross.

Yet for all of that, the principle contribution of
Luke perhaps lies elsewhere. According to the self-
conscious purpose of Luke as stated in the prologue,
he is writing a narrative of the events fulfilled in
Jesus and the early church in order to place firm
ground under the feet of Theophilus. Theophilus has
received Christian instruction (1:4, *katechein*) but
needs additional certitude and assurance. Luke's
response is to rehearse the catechesis of the church
in the form of a story of the beginnings *to the end
that Theophilus* (and Gentiles like him who have no
cognitive or existential connection to the story of
God) *may discern the larger purposes of God in past,
present and future and be confirmed in his faith
because of it.* Luke's use of special material which
is marked by the extended story form (cf. the Emmaus
account as an example) is additional evidence of his
literary approach.

What Stanley Hauerwas says of all the Gospels is
eminently true of Luke:

> The Gospels are not just the depiction of
> a man, but they are manuals for the train-
> ing necessary to be part of the new com-
> munity. To be a disciple means to share
> Christ's story, to participate in the
> reality of God's rule.[48]

Luke would agree and would say in addition that the
story of the early church is of similar if not equal

value. In Luke's mind the task of nurturing the nations into the Christian way includes the transmission of a story, God's story of saving action for the world, so that faith is not merely an isolated religious event in the individual but an event within the flow of inner and outer, personal and corporate events which locate the person in history meaningfully.

Conclusion

This survey of the nurturing activity of the early church reveals a variety and pluralism of concept and method such as one might expect in response to the various settings of church planting. At the same time the investigation has disclosed the integral connection of the nurturing approach to the spirit of the Christian faith itself. The message and the method have a symbiotic relationship.

There is an essential dynamic which appears as a constant factor throughout the various times and settings. It is the interaction of three factors that create the movement of faith nurture: a scripture which carries the normative story of faith, a people of God who model and make credible the faith, and tellers of the story who apply it for those who live at the growing edge of the story. This dynamic is the key to Christian nurture in any age.

FOOTNOTES

[1]"Education" is used here in its broadest meaning. Its root idea, still present in Italian for example, is "to lead out" with the specific connotation of "training, up-bringing." This approximates our English word "nurture" rather than formal institution learning as typical of English usage. This distinction corresponds to the usual difference made between nurture and instruction. At the same time, from an etymological standpoint, education and nurture view the matter from opposite viewpoints. "Education" arises from a socratic perspective which *educes* something latent in the person; "nurture" reflects the dependence of the child on its mother for nourishment, hence receiving from outside of the person. Both viewpoints have their place in Christian formation but perhaps "nurture" reflects more distinctively the Christian perspective--to the extent that etymology is of any consequence.

[2]Robert Ulrich, *Three Thousand Years of Educational Wisdom* (Cambridge, Mass.: Harvard University Press, 1954), p. 644. Sometimes pre-exilic and post-exilic Israel are contrasted because of the change from family nurture to formalized instruction. Leland Harder points out in a helpful way that both forms of transmitting faith have certain strengths and weaknesses. ("The Concept of Discipleship in Christian Education," *Religious Education*, Vol. LVIII, No. 4.) Here the point made by Ulrich has a validity apart from the change of method that happened in Jewish history. Reflection on the relationship of method and situation may be fruitful. See the discussion on 1 Peter below.

[3]Robert H. Stein, *The Method and Message of Jesus'
Teachings* (Phila.: Westminster, 1978), pp. 1, 2.

[4]The Apostle Paul follows a similar principle in
arguing for faith as prior to law (Gal. 3). This is
the principle which lies at the heart of the concept
of an authoritative canon of scripture. It allows the
church to return constantly to the primordial or found-
ing events of the faith for testing and guiding the
present.

[5]Philo and Josephus speak of the educational effort
by the parents to furnish a knowledge of the Torah to
their children. The Tannaitic law placed responsibility on the father for the education of his son.

[6]S. Safrai, "Education and the Study of the Torah"
in *The Jewish People in the First Century* (Section One
of *Compendium Rerum Iudaicarum ad Novum Testamentum*),
2:945-970. The description of the Jewish educational
system which follows is taken from this chapter.

[7]The presence of a "small group" method of education is of special interest in the light of present
day emphasis on this approach. According to Safrai,
op. cit., groups of various sizes met on weekday
nights or on the sabbath. One rabbi taught that every
man should find a fellow disciple (as well as a
teacher) "that he eat with him and drink with him and
read with him and learn with him." Group meals were
the setting for Torah study both in Palestine and in
the Diaspora.

> "If three have eaten at one table and have
> not spoken over it words of the Law, it is
> as though they had eaten of the sacrifice
> of the dead . . . But if three have eaten at
> one table and have spoken over it words of
> the Law, it is as if they had eaten from the
> Table of God."

Quotation taken from Safrai, p. 969.

[8] Joseph Grassi, *The Teacher in the Primitive Church and the Teacher Today* (Santa Clara, California: University of Santa Clara Press, 1973), p. 37.

[9] Within Jesus' lifetime the disciples are commissioned to heal the sick and cast out evil spirits. The evangelist Luke in particular emphasizes the place of "gospel actions" in the teaching/preaching mission. He underscores the role of signs and wonders in the early church as a continuation of the inbreaking power of the kingdom Jesus *brought and brings*.

[10] The question of the relation of present and future in Jesus' teaching of the kingdom is more complex than stated here. I am suggesting that the key point is this: the kingdom is at work in the present in such a way that a new situation is in effect demanding new responses from everyone regardless of religious, social or ethnic condition. The literature on the kingdom in Jesus' teaching is vast. One of the most recent works of value is Leonhard Goppelt, *Theology of the New Testament*, Vol. I, trans. John Alsup (Grand Rapids: Eerdmans, 1981).

[11] John W. Miller, *Step by Step Through the Parables* (New York: Paulist, 1981)., p. 6. The discussion on parables depends heavily on this book.

[12] *Ibid.*, p. 3. For a more detailed definition with emphasis on the shades of meaning of "parable" in the Gospels see Stein, *op. cit.*, p. 34-39.

[13] Archibald Hunter, "The Interpreter and the Parable: The Centrality of the Kingdom," *New Testament Issues*, ed. by Richard A. Batey (New York: Harper and Row, 1970), p. 71.

[14] It ought to be obvious that "historical" is used in contrast to "metaphorical" and does not speak to the question of ancient versus modern scientific historiography. It refers to narrative that describes its object directly rather than analogously.

[15]Robert C. Tannehill emphasizes this point in his study of the synoptic sayings. "I have come to believe that some of the characteristics which . . . scholars attribute to the parable, or to metaphor, apply broadly to other types of forceful and imaginative language in the Gospels." They are "able to jolt the hearer out of familiar continuities into a new judgment about existence." *The Sword of His Mouth* (Phila.: Fortress Press, 1975), p. 2.

[16]J. A. Fitzmyer, *The Gospel According to Luke*, Anchor Bible (New York: Doubleday, 1981), 1:148.

[17]Admittedly these features have been implicated in the issues of editorial interest of the evangelist, especially the Messianic secret problem in Mark. There is enough evidence from tradition history study and from the intrinsic probabilities of the setting in Jesus' life to suppose that we have here a reflection of things as they really were in the original setting.

[18]Compare the emphasis with the Sermon on the Mount that the world will be called to God by the city on the hill (people of God) and the good works of the disciples. The very event of the sermon illustrates the principle! This close relationship between *kerygma* and *didache* leads to the observation, significant for Anabaptist theology, that salvation and ethics are inseparable, that evangelism and discipleship are interrelated.

[19]"Teaching," *New International Dictionary of New Testament Theology*, (Grand Rapids: Zondervan, 1978), 3:765.

[20]Thomas H. Groome, *Christian Religious Education: Sharing Our Story and Vision* (New York: Harper and Row, 1980), p. 265.

[21]*Ibid.*, p. 266.

79

[22]*Ibid.*, p. 265. The distinction between teaching and prophecy is even more difficult to ascertain with certainty. The best explanation is that teaching was characterized by instruction in the traditions of scripture, Jesus, and earlier Christians (see further in main text). Prophecy was the more spontaneous insight into the Spirit's direction, correction, or prediction for the church's good in the present decision making. See David Hill, *New Testament Prophecy* (Atlanta: John Knox, 1979).

[23]For a powerful illustration see Paul's argument in Galatians 2:11-21 *from* the "kerygmatic" truth of justification by faith in Jesus Christ *to* the "didactic" truth of full fellowship at the Lord's Table between the Jew and Greek.

[24]It also makes the lists of virtues (Haustafeln) in the epistles vulnerable to the critical judgment that they are unintegrated borrowings from current philosophical or religious traditions—which they may well be from a purely formal point of view.

[25]K. H. Rengstorf, "didasko, . . .," *Theological Dictionary of the New Testament* (Grand Rapids: Eerdmans, 1964), 2:145.

[26]We cannot enter into the complex question of how the tradition process influenced the transmission of Jesus' teaching although there can be no doubt that the Jesus traditions which we do have in the New Testament writings were preserved and handed on in a manner similar to the Jewish practices. We will be wrong to assume, however, that the disciples saw themselves as learners who would become masters—Jesus always remained the living Lord and Master. Moreover (and consistent with the preceding) the disciples did not treat Jesus' teaching as a dead deposit of truth. It had a living quality parallel to the living Lord who mediates the past to the present himself. See 1 Corinthians 11:23 where Paul makes Jesus the subject of

the tradition process! On the whole subject see, for
the latest review of scholarship, James D. G. Dunn,
Unity and Diversity in the New Testament (Phila.:
Westminster, 1977), pp. 60-80.

[27]*Ibid.*, p. 66.

[28]Richard Longenecker, *Biblical Exegesis in the
Apostolic Period* (Grand Rapids, Eerdmans, 1975) and
Dunn, *op. cit.* pp. 81-102.

[29]See the works cited in the previous note.

[30]Dunn, *op. cit.*, p. 68.

[31]The word "practice" in this heading carries the
significance carried in recent discussion of educational philosophy by the word "praxis," that is, the
interaction of theoretical reflection and concrete
action.

[32]J. Elliott, *A Home for the Homeless* (Phila.:
Fortress Press, 1981), p. 13 citing Goppelt, *Der
erste Petrusbrief* , p. 41. Elliott's book is a significant source for this entire section.

[33]*Ibid.*, p. 270.

[34]*Ibid.*, p. 284-288.

[35]See Elliott's interesting discussion based on
Robert Nisbet, *The Social Philosophers: Community
and Conflict in Western Thought.* He believes that the
familial and household self-consciousness of the
Petrine community is the one most characteristic and
distinctive features. Nisbet claims that the family
constituted a more formidable barrier to the advance
of Christianity than did the general socio-political
structure. Thus the establishment of the claims of
the household of God over the physical kinship. This
picture would be consistent with Jesus' own words in
Matt. 10:34-39; Mark 3:31-35; and Luke 14:25-26 which

set the disciple call over family loyalty. This probably explained the relative absence of reliance on the biological family as a means of Christian nurture (but see Eph. 6:4). The first generation situation saw the family as an obstacle to conversion, not yet as a means of promoting and transmitting faith.

[36]Ralph P. Martin, *The Family and the Fellowship: New Testament Images of the Church* (Grand Rapids: Eerdmans, 1979), pp. 123-125.

[37]For the development and application of the perspective see the chapter by Larry Richards on 'Christian Education of the Church Today and Tomorrow" and "The Body of Christ: God's Setting for Learning the Bible" in *Future Church*, ed. Ralph W. Neighbor, Jr. (Nashville: Broadman Press, 1980.

[38]"Teaching, "admonishing" and "singing" are modal participles defining the means by which the dwelling of the word takes place.

[39]It is true that the words for teaching and admonishing appear together often in general usage. See Lohse, *Colossians and Philemon*, Hermenia Commentary (Phila.: Fortress Press, 1971), p. 77. But the presence of *nouthetein* (rebuke, warn, set right) does color the whole expression.

[40]The terms used for the singing--psalms, hymns and spiritual songs--defy exact definition or distinction but clearly speak of that spontaneous, Spirit inspired worship in which individuals and the group became participants in the communication. *Ibid.*, p. 151.

[41]The purpose here is not to reduce thanksgiving to an intropsychic phenomenon with no real God-ward movement. The point is to note that the attitude of dependency, openness, and celebration involved in gratitude is at the same time the attitudes that promote the appropriation of spiritual truth.

[42]P. Bonnard, "Matthieu Educateur du peuple chrétien" in *Mélange Biblique en hommage au B. Regaux*. Quoted by Ralph P. Martin, *New Testament Foundations*, Vol. I (Grand Rapids: Eerdmans, 1975), p. 242.

[43]The term "scribe" is a Jewish term and its use reflects the Jewish flavor of this Gospel. The Jewish scribe was, in our parlance, the teacher-theologian. This role that unites teacher and theologian brings to mind Groome's complaint that in contrast to the early church the church today has separated the educational and theological ministries. (*Christian Religious Education*, p. 229.)

[44]R. P. Martin, *op. cit.*, p. 230. Krister Stendahl's suggestion that a school of interpretation in the style of Qumran stands behind Matthew's Gospel is probably incorrect. Rather what seems likely is that the Christian congregation sees itself functioning as a disciple group continuing the disciple band of Jesus and using the style and methods of the several Jewish rabbinic, synagogal and sectarian traditions in imitation of Jesus or as appropriate to their consciousness as a messianic community.

[45]*Ibid.*, p. 230.

[46]*Ibid.*, p. 242.

[47]For detail see, for example, Xavier Léon-Dufour, *The Gospels and the Jesus of History* (Garden City, New York: Doubleday. Image Books, 1970), pp. 119-121.

[48]Stanely Hauerwas, *A Community of Character* (Notre Dame, Ind.: University of Notre Dame Press, 1981), p. 49.

RESPONSES TO PAPER

Mark Derstine: Although George said that there is a paucity of New Testament texts that speak about educational methodology, I'd like to express appreciation for all that comes out of this paper with significance for the nurturing of faith. The first point that touched me was the comment that nurture takes place in the context of a counter-community developing an alternative value system. Assuming the accurateness of that interpretation of the New Testament setting (not to mention our own Anabaptist origins in the Radical Reformation), my concern about that is the conservative mood in which we now view ourselves as separate from and out of the world, at least as indicated by my own personal experience of growing up in the Franconia Conference. To be sure, I grew up in a "counter community" with concern for being separate from the world; but we defined it in terms of different dress—the plain clothes that my parents and all of their generation wore. The main concern for developing alternate elementary and high schools in our Conference was keeping separate and maintaining different value systems and holding to the faith. I valued a lot of that as I attended those schools, but in time I also became aware that the way in which we were different lacked the context of discovering what new and joyful life in Christ there really is alternative to the ways of the larger society. Our attitude in relation to society was defensive rather than the more joyful kind of following Christ in terms of newness of life and community—a "moral majority" kind of reaction to what is viewed as offensive out there and defining oneself in terms of what one is against. There is a growing debate in our communities as to how much we have become comfortable as part of the comfort of the larger society, and whether or not here is still another way we can really be "in the world and yet not of the world"—in a way that we continue to be aware of our distinctive differentness from the world but yet in a much more positive sense of modeling something over and against the world that is inviting to the world rather than that which we have to hold onto and protect ourselves against. Consequently, the self-preservation concern is no longer as dominant as it was in my younger life experience, and we're beginning to work at that self-preservation problem in a different way.

My second point related to the emphasis on teaching by example. Again, I sense an acute contrast between the importance of this to Jesus in his own teaching ministry not only in relation to his disciple group but to the larger community, and our own congregational teaching structures, in which it is so difficult to see that life modeled in our Sunday school and preaching settings. To be sure, there are a lot of words that are still holding before us the ideal standards of life in Christ, but it's so hard to see how they might be lived out in a practical kind of way. Hence, the comment that was made in our last session about the cynicism of our youth in terms of seeing our practice as being consistent with our message. I think we're working on that by trying various discipling methods, like the discipling model for learning and growing into spiritual maturity at Eastern Mennonite Seminary, the Paul-Timothy program in certain conferences and the Life Planning program of matching adults with youth.

My third response concerns the bridging of the kerygma and didache and the comment that the teaching of ethics should not be separated from the kerygma. Again from my own experience, I would have to say that the emphasis in my home community on following Jesus was very serious but lacked the experience of grace, and we need to discover how grace was the source of that following and that discipleship. Without grace, that comes through largely as legalistic command; and a lot of walls are raised very quickly.

Finally, I found the comments about the church as a familial community very helpful as a model for our own worship and education. This concept that our congregation is a family of God that can unite married people and single persons and children as well as elderly persons is a potentially great image. This raises the question about where children's nurture best takes place, and unfortunately the New Testament documents do not help us much on that question, except by implication. Perhaps if church is truly a family of God in the New Testament sense of coming together as a depth community, our children learn the Christian mysteries simply by being a part of these. Still, we need to talk more of the specific responsibilities of parents in modern settings in which nuclear family members are scattered and not coming together in spiritual family settings as frequently as might be true in more intentional kinds of communities in which ways are found to recreate the neighborhood base for spiritual family nurture.

Elizabeth Yoder: In some ways I found myself identifying more with the models presented out of the New Testament than out of the Old Testament. And I found that sort of surprising since I'm the same age as some of you who responded to the Old Testament paper. As I reflected on this, I decided it was because of the emphasis placed in this paper on the church as a counter-culture. The church into which I was born was more like the Old Testament community in the sense that it was more a community where all the values were shared by everyone around. Then when I was six we moved to a community where my father was pastor of a small church and where there were less than one hundred Mennonites. There I had a stronger feeling that the church was a counter-culture and that we were different from everyone else in town. I suspect that our rural Mennonite communities were more like the Old Testament community than the New Testament situation in our reliance on the family and clan for passing on values.

Now, however, most of us find ourselves in urban settings where our church and family values are in direct conflict with those other people around us. I often tell my children that we're raising them to swim against the stream. They don't particularly like that. They say that's all right for us, but it's hard for kids. For me in my youth, swimming against the stream meant things like dress and hair style and not being able to do certain things that all the other kids did, but for my children it's not the same thing. So, I identify with some of the things that Mark said about ethics needing to grow out of our joy, not being a legalistic sort of thing.

Now I'm a member of a small house church, and in a sense I think a house church is a counter-culture to the sanctuary-type church; so that's another way in which we see ourselves to be something different. I really identified with the statement, "The church possesses a keen self-identity and, at the same time, is intensely involved in the structures of the larger society." That really characterizes our own house church in the sense that we see ourselves as counter-culture in relationship to other churches, even Mennonite churches; but at the same time we try to be intensely involved in what is going on in society. We're concerned about nuclear proliferation, we're concerned about poverty and injustice all around the world--types of things the Mennonite communities of the past did not particularly concern themselves with.

Other things in this paper I found very stimulating, although I'm less ready to make many pronouncements about, are the lack of reliance on the biological family as a means of Christian nurture (how we view that) and the idea that Jesus was a re-visionist, a change agent, not just somebody who gathered the wisdom of the past and made reforms, but somebody who was radically different in his approach.

Don Miller: I had almost the opposite reaction to this paper than I did to the one this morning. This morning I was wishing that there had been more attention to the variety of responses of the Hebrew community to what was going on, because the presentation gave the impression that there was a single kind of response when I suspect that one could make the case for a variety of responses. In this paper, the variety so overwhelms me that I can't find the unity. In spite of the fact that it opens by talking about the counter-community and closes with a reference to the integral connection between a radical faith and the nurturing methods of the faith community, referred to as the real nub of the

matter, I don't think that either of these references do justice to the variety
that's covered in the paper itself. I think the conclusion covers over a lot of
what was said in the paper which was so rich with possibilities that perhaps the
conclusion should have been left off so that one doesn't forget the many kinds
of things that were said in the paper itself.

Now that leads me to comment that in our work in education, there's a
tendency to want to drive through to a single principle of education; and what
I come away with in this paper is to see that in the New Testament you can't do
that. There's such a variety that to drive it through to one principle just
doesn't work. I was so taken by the way George treated the kerygma-didache
approach, and he tried to show that you just can't break the material easily into
one or the other type, but that each type includes the other. I was so taken by
that because our tendency all the time is to dichotomize these, which especially
serves a sacramental church tradition because by emphasizing the Word/preaching
as sacrament, one has first to preach the Word in the church, and teaching
becomes secondary and nonsacramental. One catches this peril within our own
ecclesiology also, and hence it's so important to reinterpret what's going on
here as George did in this paper. I got the impression that the New Testament
writers were driven to those kerygmatic formulas by treating first certain
didactic [educational] questions they were working at and then giving kerygmatic
foundation to the answers they gave in their teaching. Those today who stress
so much the kerygmatic side seem to suggest that it's first of all kerygma and
then if they move on to teaching, that is quite incidental.

I just finished work on a book entitled, *Contemporary Approaches to Christian Education* [co-authored with Jack Seymour, Abingdon Press, 1982, 176 pp.]
and I suggested five different models of Christian education that dominate right
now. One is an instruction approach, focused on the school. Another is a
community approach , focused on the hidden curriculum of the life of the community. The third is the developmental approach, which features the process of
maturing in the faith. The fourth is the liberation approach, which features
changes in the structures of society. And the last one is the interpretation-
approach, which features the revelation and reinterpretation of our life according to God's presence. Now those are different approaches, and the interesting
thing about George's paper is how he made a case for every single one of them.
He talked about the schools in the tradition. He looked at the Pauline-Colossian
material in relation to the familial community approach. He talked about the
Holy Spirit as basic and made a good case for the development approach in
talking about maturing toward faith and salvation as a life-process. He had a
splendid section on Jesus as the revisionist--re-visionist--which makes the case
for a liberation approach, although I wish he had made that more pervasive than
just only at one point. Then he had a strong section about reinterpretation,
but all these points don't easily fit together. There are big fights among educators about which is the proper approach. Re-visioning is unhappy with the
developmental view and tries to throw it out. A community approach isn't happy
with the school approach, and an educator like John Westerhoff with his community
approach wants to do away with the school, which is allegedly not doing us any
service anymore. So, it's nice to see them all listed here; but I want more help.
Which way are we going to go? We have roots in all of these possibilities, it
seems to me. I would want to point out the way that they not only are there,
but that they also conflict with each other.

It seems to me that one of the things we do in education is to work with
the symbols of faith--the deepest insights into revelation that we have--and to
work at their reinterpretation for ourselves, i.e., the fifth approach. We can't
teach the faith in a form that will stay put. We teach it as well as we can and
then rejoice when they reinterpret it.

Related to this is the point George made about the family. On one hand, we
use a family image for our Christian nurture; but on the other hand, as in the

I Peter material, the family image stands in the way. So what we need is not simply a family image, but what could be called a "new family" image, i.e., not just a kinship family, closest to our hearts, but a faith family, or a new family image.

Take the matter of modeling. The problem with the modeling-model is that no one of us is good enough to be a model; and therefore, there's something audacious about stressing a modeling image of education. I recall that when they came to Jesus and said, "Good teacher, what must I do to inherit eternal life?", he said, "Now, wait a minute; there's no one good but God alone. Don't start that way with me." And so the modeling approach might start by denying that there's a modeling approach, which has its own peculiar kind of problem.

And so my concluding comment is that this paper is rich with possibilities and varieties but leaves us with a lot of questions about how things fit together.

PLENARY DISCUSSION

Leland Harder: Before we open the discussion to the whole group, perhaps we should give Waldemar and George an opportunity to reply to the responses that have just been made to both papers so far. Waldemar, do you want to respond to Don's question about whether education in the Old Testament was as unified as your paper seemed to imply?

Waldemar Janzen: I think I would have to hear a little more about what kind of diversity Don has in mind.

Donald Miller: I could give a couple of examples. When one looks at the history of the kings, for instance, one gets two different accounts of it, and they don't easily harmonize with each other. Or one could point to the diversity of interpretations of a given theme in the Old Testament; and it seemed to me that you drew them together in a way that made it seem that there was such a nice unitary pattern in all of it. The reason I raised the question about it is that we are so taken with the varieties of our own situation that it would be enormously helpful to look at the varieties in the Old Testament to see how that was being worked at in their nurture and instruction as a way for us to better comprehend our own varieties.

Waldemar Janzen: First of all, I think in any one paper like mine, one must immediately plead guilty to over-simplification. But having said that, I am deliberately countering a trend at work in Old Testament studies--the disjoining trend. You have a Chroniclist school, and you have a Deuternomist school, each functioning for certain purposes; but when I go to Palestine and look from one mountain and see half the country before me, and I think that even when we make some of our major distinctions like between priests, wise men, prophets, etc., or between the northern and southern kingdoms and theologies, or between the Mosaic covenant and the Levitic covenant, etc., I get a common-sense hunch that they were all a little more together and mixed up than much Old Testament scholarship allows. But you may be right that I was leaning over against that so much that I went overboard in the other direction of unity. But I thought I had three perspectives on the nurture of youth, not just one; and at least in that section I tried to differentiate.

Leland Harder: Now let's turn to George for his replies.

George Brunk: I have two comments. The first refers to what Mark was saying about the problem of an alternate value system, and I simply want to point us again in the direction of what I was attempting to disclose in I Peter. We see a picture there of an alternate community that was very much in contact with the larger cultural setting of which it was a part; and I would suggest that

e kind of counter-community position you see there requires a kind of educa-
ion that nurtures people in the knowledge of the world along with the knowledge
$ the faith, because that is the only way in which we can truly live a dynamic
unter-position in the larger society. That is something to which we have been
inded in the older Mennonite community, although we certainly have overcome
at in the educational process more recently. But maybe we have lost some of the
ility to hold these two together in the kind of tension we see in I Peter.
d we certainly have to work harder at this than the larger monolithic society in
ts educational process. I am often impressed by the fact that the American
ciety, for example, can rely so massively on the informal structures of life to
ansmit its values. Precisely because it stands over against the larger society,
e church needs to take deliberate steps to counter the informal conditioning
wers of the larger society; and that's why we need to take some deliberate
rmal steps to work against that which we are rejecting. So I would argue for a
ry positive way of living that alternate value system and work back to I Peter.

In response to Don, I would say that he was just plain keen in his observa-
ons that my paper brings out a great variety of models; and this says something
out the conception I had of the paper itself, that it should emphasize a des-
iptive rather than a prescriptive approach. Waldemar was more courageous when
 concluded with his six points; and I laud him for that. I think that's prob-
ly appropriate. I didn't push myself either to answer Don's question about
at one would reach for in terms of the unity of the models, or unifying model,
at emerges from the New Testament. This probably reflects an assumption of
ne that if there is diversity of nurturing models in the New Testament, that
 going to have to correspond to a diversity that has to exist in our own situ-
ion. But how do we live with diversity when there are only two or three pub-
shing houses that have to supply curricula for all of us? How can we allow
at kind of openness to exist and yet seek a model that has local integrity? I
ink I would still want to come back to my closing statement concerning a kind
 constant dynamic that has implications for the ongoing task of Christian
rture, although I wouldn't try to derive out of that any final model. It
esn't contain that final model, you're right; but what I'm suggesting is that
 you want a criterion for what is Christian nurture, you can still say that you
ve a people who are living the story, however frail; and they have ways of
pturing that story in the Scriptures, and in their history and some of their
aditions in a secondary way. Those are the constants that I see, and that
uld be about the most criterion that I would want to lift out of the New Testa-
nt in testing any model.

Leland Harder: Now before we break up again into groups, let's take a few
nutes for additional questions and observations, while they are fresh in our
nds.

Bertha Harder: You didn't speak to Mark's last question about where
ildren's nurture comes in. Is that important in the New Testament?

George Brunk: Yes, I assumed that question would come up again and be
arpened a bit. There was some discussion on this during the coffee break, and
d like to emphasize one point concerning this. I think we have to recognize
certain historical given in the case of the New Testament, and that is that it
es not embrace a time span that one would call truly intergenerational. To be
re, you have texts with intergenerational application, like the exhortation to
e fathers to nurture their children. You have the reference to Timothy's
tergenerational background. But overall, one has to be impressed with the
ct that the biological family does not seem to be involved in or geared up for
e process of Christian nurture. Now I would assume that the strong emphasis
 the family as the model of community life together included the expectation
at the children were part of that whole process and were absorbing all that was
rt of the family of God. But I also suspect that not all of the concerns of an
going transmission of the faith emerged within the time frame of the New Testa-

ment documents. The ones that do represent second generation would be principally the Matthew and Luke documents, to which I gave attention; and there you can at least begin to see an awareness of what it's going to take to involve new generations in Kingdom living. Luke is aware of the fact that he is second and not third generation. He looks back with nostalgia on the witnesses of the Word who gathered all this information and gave it to us. Now how do we get it out to all those Theophiluses who are in the third generation? Well, his whole writing in two parts is an illustration of how he goes about doing this. But you do not read very much there concerning the family dynamics of doing that.

The other point I want to make is simply to underscore what I alluded to with respect to the relationship of the spiritual family to the biological family. On one hand, the New Testament use of the family metaphor implies that the spiritual family does have priority over the biological family; but on the other hand, the biological family aspires to use the dynamics of the family to be itself, to grow, to propagate itself, and to promote the welfare of its members. The extension of this would be for the church to recruit the biological family to do the job of Christian nurture and formation; and I think the whole New Testament points in the direction of saying to the biological family to do it, and to do it with all its might, seeing the family and the church as partners while recognizing that there will be a degree of tension between the spiritual family and the biological family, especially where the church needs to have a counter-community stance in society.

Ross Bender: You made reference to Ephesians 6:4 concerning the exhortation to fathers to bring up their children in the discipline and instruction of the Lord, but you did not elaborate on it. Do you see that as a harking back to the Old Testament principle that Waldemar talked about this morning, or is that just an isolated reference?

George Brunk: My feeling would be that both of your comments are correct, that it reflects the Old Testament roots of the new community to say that the children ought to be the responsibility of the parent, but also that the nurture of children was not in the forefront of concern at the time of the early church. We simply have to recognize that we don't get much concrete help on how to nurture our children in the faith, although the New Testament certainly points in the direction of the prior responsibility of the biological family.

Leland Harder: We have to break at this point if we're going to have our group discussions this afternoon. As we do so and in spite of Waldemar's admonition, I'd like to encourage the small groups to draw out of these papers so far the practical implications for a renewed vision for congregational education today.

SMALL GROUP REPORTS

Paul Unruh: A good bit of focus in our group was on whether or not the church really sees itself as a counter-culture. If it begins to take that seriously, there are some rather broad implications for church nurture, especially in view of the strong influence which the world has upon our people, children as well as adults. One implication is that nurture must happen on a multi-level basis and in partnership between family, a small faith community, and the larger congregation. We had a rather emphatic statement or two that the nuclear family cannot handle the task alone, but that something like a mentor system or a convenanting kind of system is needed to assist the partnership.

Helmut Harder: Group #6 focused on two questions: What is it that is to be transmitted? And what is the goal of our transmission. When George mentioned "fundamentals" in passing, some of our people heard that and said, "Now, there's

where we need to zero in. What are these fundamentals?" And related to that,
what is the end or goal of our nurturing? We moved from that to a related concern, and that is, what did Jesus bring that was new, that was good, that was
better? And the upshot of that was that we added a fourth factor to the concluding paragraph of George's paper. In addition to "a scripture which carries
the normative story of faith, a people of God who model and make credible the
faith, and tellers of the story who apply it for those who live at the growing
edge of the story," we said we also need the Holy Spirit; and there was a strong
"Yea" and "Amen."

James Schrag: As nearly as I can recall, our group talked about two things.
The first had to do with the diversity-of-models part of the discussion, and the
feeling of our group was that diversity is basically a positive quality. In fact,
we felt there's a danger of exclusiveness among us, of focusing too narrowly on
one or two ways of nurturing the faith. Some illustrations were given along
this line of models we felt were potentially destructive to the Christian community and ones to watch out for. The second question pertained to the biological
family versus the spiritual family, and which takes priority. Is there a tension between our rhetoric of giving priority to the spiritual family and our
practice of expressing our loyalty to the biological family? My own editorial
comment from a pastor's point of view is to observe the attendance at ballgames
versus the attendance at church functions and to ask, which one is the primary
family and which the extended family? Is the church the extended family? Or is
it the primary family?

Levi Miller: Group #3 had two concerns. The first, already mentioned by
group #4, is the question of whether we should really move toward one model or
design of Christian nurture, and the other pertains to the meaning of nurture
itself. We looked ahead to the agenda for tomorrow night with the title, "Toward
an Intergenerational Design of Christian Education;" and we thought that was
baiting the question somewhat and was already naming the design when the assignment of the papers was broader than this and we've already heard considerable
affirmation for a variety of models. We want to work toward a design but not
give it a name as yet. Perhaps it will include several designs or models. Our
second question was on the use of the word, "nurture." We felt that either it
needs redefinition or we need a new term to describe our enterprise. The word
seems to imply in-group perpetuation, and we want a term that implies reaching
out to persons in the world who really want to be a part of a counter-community.
It was an evangelism concern that was spoken to here. But then we came to the
thought that perhaps nurture implies informal education as its key ingredient,
and that as such it also includes the evangelistic thrust.

John Rogers: Four questions came out of group #2. One would be the need
to be counter-cultural in creative, empowering ways, not only for the counter-
community but also for the broader community. The second point: we questioned
to what degree the counter-cultural model implies that God is not working in the
broader community. Should we perhaps accept the possibility that God is in fact
working in the broader community and therefore the counter-community also has to
look beyond itself to understand what God is going in history? Third, we found
an implication in the paper for teacher-training, namely, that it is not simply or
primarily a methodological consideration but we're looking at such things as ideas,
values, and world view--the idea that we have to move teachers toward a model of
Jesus as teacher of the kingdom of God. And the fourth concern was that although
there was little concern for the education of children as such, the providing of
an educational context, i.e., a counter-community, has significant implications
for the nurture of children.

Dick Rempel: We talked a lot in our group about modeling as a form of nurture. We appreciated Don Miller's comment that modeling is not the only way, that
Jesus himself put this in a larger perspective, that a model does not have to be
perfect since only God is perfect. The model is a teacher who is being changed;

and that might open us all to God's grace to be models worthy of pointing to the perfect model. In this sense, the whole congregation with multiple models of Christian nurture is itself a model that can bring wholeness to what faith and life is all about. Thus, the varieties of Christian education make for a more holistic growth and faith. Others in the community of faith help our children to grow up in the faith.

Leland Harder: Before we adjourn in preparation for the third section of our schedule this evening, I think we should ask the task force and Ross Bender in particular, who had the responsibility of writing up the design for this workshop, whether they have any response to the concern of group #4 that we presupposed the outcome of this seminar-workshop.

Ross Bender: Well, I must say that I'm delighted that it's producing considerable discussion and debate. Our idea of setting up a design to be tested was not meant to be selling something but to be testing it; and we're getting some clear soundings to this point that one model is not adequate. I think that part of our intention was to say precisely that with respect to the schooling model: it is not adequate. And so we set up another to test that; and perhaps both approaches together--the socialization approach and the instruction approach--are not adequate. That's the point of testing.

In any case, we did not get our design written. Whether it was just the accident of climate or whatever, but John Gaeddert swooped into town one day a few weeks ago when we were going to work on it, hovered a few feet above the runway, and decided to take off again for points north. So the task force did not get to meet, and now we're going to do that between each session, gathering the input from the papers and from the responses and group reports, and trying to sift all of that to see what are the assumptions that go into our designing Christian education approaches that will be superior, I'm sure, to any pre-packaged thing that some of you were feeling unhappy about, fearing that you were being invited to come to a conference where the conclusions were already written before you came. That's a misunderstanding of our intentions; but even if it had been our intention, we didn't quite pull it off. So we're going to have to struggle together to hear what emerges from the process and look at that and test it together; and I'm pleased that it got you here and got you excited and mad enough to want to debate. So here we are together, looking at a couple of approaches, one that we have more or less taken for granted--the schooling approach--and the other one that we're trying to set up here over against it: the socialization or intergenerational approach; and we're finding that the diversity of approaches is even greater. I don't think that means just smorgasbord. I think we have to put our discriminating and discerning faculties to work here to ask what is it about our situation that can guide us concerning the way we go about nurturing the faith and which of these several models can best serve us in our time.

It is clear at this stage of our seminar that the answers are not in yet on that. I must state this: I doubt that they'll be in by the end of this conference; and I won't be disappointed. But I think we will have advanced in our insight into the issues, and I'm hopeful that there will be a second seminar a year from now, and maybe a third in two years, as we work together to find the best ways in their time to carry on the task of education and nurture.

Leland Harder: I would want to add my warning to Ross' that you have only heard one-fourth of the papers so far; and if you think we have experienced multiplicity of models so far, just wait until we get to the ninth century this evening and to the sixteenth century tomorrow morning, and to the twentieth century tomorrow afternoon.

A PATRISTIC AND MEDIEVAL PERSPECTIVE

Peter C. Erb

The locus of education for the patristic and medieval church was not the school nor the family, nor the "congregation" and certainly not the "nation," but the *church*. The person chiefly responsible for the well-being of the church's "care of souls" (the medieval term for "nurture") was the bishop, the pastor. When medieval and patristic authors wrote treatises on education they were concerned with the centre of the process as they saw it, but did not by so doing ignore the rest of the society. The healthy education of the church (they could not think of a radically reduced, separated self-existent form of that church as we do of our congregations) depended on the health of the teacher.

It is not possible within the space allotted to me by the Creator--much less by the strictures of this essay) to provide even a brief outline of Christian education in the patristic and medieval periods. Together, these two periods make up three-quarters of Christian history and include, aside from the first century, the most significant Christian epoch (Nicea, 325 AD, to Chalcedon, 451 AD). We are concerned here with fourteen hundred years of spirituality, with the reflections and judgements of forty-two generations of Christians compared with a mere twelve generations of analysis and study since the Reformation era.

The temporal scope is not the only difficulty faced by a surveyor of this period. Much of the evidence documenting Christian life during the patristic and medieval centuries remains unedited, even more is unread, and relatively little is fully interpreted.[1]

More problematic still are the prejudices which shape
many Christian attitudes to these ages. Even after a
century and a half of careful scholarship, for example,
Christians at large still share with their secular
colleagues the seemingly unquestioned assumption that
the years here under discussion are a vast ignorant,
superstitious dark *middle* ages lying somehow between
pure primitive Christianity and the glory and grandeur
of classical civilisation on the one hand and, on the
other, a corrected "biblical" religion (Protestant
Reformation) and a renewed progressive view of free
human potential (Renaissance). A critique of this negative view of the middle ages will become evident as
this paper proceeds.

The problem of treating such extensive material can
be met in only one way. I have chosen not to offer a
survey of approaches to Christian education; the state
of contemporary scholarship and certainly of my own
knowledge makes this impossible. Rather I have judged
it useful to analyse one text in detail and to do so by
allowing it to represent the age, to serve as a mirror
reflecting the peculiar questions and answers of its
own world as well as those of the world out of which it
arose. This image of the text as mirror is a medieval
commonplace (its later use by Marxists ought not to
prejudice its use); but the medievals were wise enough
to realise that as a mirror a text not only reflects
its own and earlier times, but the time of the reader
as well. In ancient texts we see ourselves more clearly.

The world described in this paper is different from
our modern world and to understand it requires a change
of thought which can only take place after slow reflection. As a result I have chosen to *introduce* the tra-
vellor to the terrain rather than provide a tourist
with a guide to the main roads. I have centered my
attention on one text, a preface of Alfred the Great to
his translation of Pope Gregory the Great's *Pastoral
Care* because Alfred faced most clearly a major crisis
in the medieval church: the possibility that in

is kingdom Christian life could be overcome and van-
quished, that because of its inability to develop proper
approaches to Christian education, memory of it might be
lost forever. That there is an analogy between Alfred's
age and our own is, for me, a fact; that we might overcome our crises is not so obvious.

Since I am dealing in great detail with one specific
text, I have appended a translation of that text to this
paper. The reader may wish to study the translation
closely before turning to the paper.

. Alfred's "Preface" to *The Pastoral Care*[2]

We begin then with a simple two-page document, a
preface written by the ninth-century English king,
Alfred the Great, to an Anglo-Saxon version of Pope
Gregory the Great's sixth-century treatise, *The Pastoral
Care*. When Alfred came to the throne in 871, England
had been suffering greatly from Danish Viking raiders
for some seventy years, and the pagan Danes were in
control of almost all the country except the south-west
area of Wessex. After a long period of war the Danes
were defeated and christianised. Peace was eventually
established in 887, and Alfred turned his attention to
domestic problems, first among which was education.
Self-conscious about his own lack of education, Alfred
reestablished monastery schools and formed a school in
his own household. Concerned about the lack of learning
he directed the translations of major works, the *Soli-
oquies* of St. Augustine, Boethius' *Consolation of Philosophy*, Pope Gregory the Great's *Dialogues* and *Pastoral
Care*, and the Venerable Bede's *Ecclesiastical History
of the English Speaking Peoples*.

Alfred's translation of Gregory's *Pastoral Care* is
prefaced with a letter to bishop Waerferth in which the
king calls to mind earlier and more prosperous times.
In 597 Augustine of Canterbury had landed in Kent and
begun the conversion of the Anglo-Saxons. By the middle of the following century the conversion of England
was almost completed and for the next century Christian

culture and learning flourished on the island. The
period saw the work of the monastic scholars Benedict
Biscop (d. 689), Aldhelm (d. 709), Bede (d. 735) and
Alcuin (d. 804), the saints Cuthbert (d. 687), Wilfrid
(d. 709), Guthlac (d. 714), Ceolfrid (d. 716) and
others, and the missionary endeavours on the continent
by Boniface (d. 754). Those were prosperous times for
England, Alfred recalls. Kings were then obedient to
God and his servants and maintained peace, morality
and order. Wisdom flourished and pastors were zealous
to study, teach and fulfill the duties to which they
were ordained. So well-known was England's scholarship
that many came from foreign lands to seek it.

But such is no longer the case, Alfred laments.
Now the English must seek learning elsewhere than in
their own lands. When Alfred came to the throne few
could understand or read their prayerbooks in Latin.
It is only thanks to God that there are any teachers
remaining. Because of this situation, Alfred asks the
bishop to apply himself to wisdom. We must consider,
he writes, the punishment which would arise if the
present generation neither loved wisdom nor allowed
later generations to love it. The lamentable decline
of learning is the direct result of the Viking raids
(beginning 793), but Alfred is not willing to find its
source in those raids. He recalls that even before
the Vikings had come, when the churches were filled
with books and there were many pastors, knowledge had
fallen away. The pastors of that day recognized their
ignorance, an ignorance of the language of the books
themselves; the volumes were written in Latin, not in
the vernacular Anglo-Saxon. But both Alfred and the
pastors he characterizes know well that their lack of
Latin learning is no excuse, and he portrays them as
commenting on their ancestors' efforts positively, not
negatively. He does not describe them as blaming their
ancestors for not translating the works so that they
might be read by all. The ignorant pastors have wisdom enough to know that it was a deliberated act on
the part of their fathers not to translate. The

fathers did not translate because they wished that
'the more wisdom would be in the land, the more we
understand languages" (literal translation). Wisdom
itself could be transferred only in the original
language, not aside from it. And yet Alfred knew that
the Hebrew canon had been translated into Greek, the
Hebrew and Greek Scriptures into Latin, and part of
the Scriptures into the languages of other peoples as
well. On this precedent, and this precedent alone,
Alfred arrives at a striking conclusion: to translate
the *most needful* books into Anglo-Saxon. He softens
his suggestion with the comment that "it seems better"
to him to do so if the bishop agrees. His request for
eccelsiastical approval is natural, but what is the
alternative of translating books better than? It cannot be better than leaving them in the original, because Alfred has already cited positively the fathers'
decision not to translate. To this question of the
better way we will return, but we can do so only
after reflecting on a number of aspects of Alfred's
program.

2. Community and Persuasive Form

Our discussion may seem somewhat distant from the
theme of the seminar, namely, Christian education, and
it is well to remind ourselves of Alfred's intention.
The selection reviewed above is a preface to what was
perhaps the most important educational treatise in the
middle ages, *The Pastoral Care* of Gregory the Great. [3]
Pope Gregory's work does not begin as would a modern
work on the same topic with a study of educational
technique. Technique is directed to the student, the
one to be taught. Nor does it begin with content, the
material to be transposed to the student by the technique. Rather, Gregory attends to the teacher (for him
the pastor-bishop as the image of the whole church and
not the local priest), and not to the teacher's know-
edge but to his being , to the manner in which he came
to his position, (unworthy inspiration leads to an unworthy teacher) to the manner of his life in it, to
his manner of teaching, and to his humility in teaching.

The salvific wisdom of Christianity is incarnated,
passed on by people not by information retrieval systems or techniques of interpersonal dynamics. Moreover, such wisdom is passed on in a community; and to
the bishop as the primary image of that community falls
the responsibility for its transmission. It may strike
us as strange that the primary focus of pastoral care
(radically distinct from pastoral counseling) is learning (education); but that strangeness, as we will soon
see, is alone the result of our peculiar reduction of
learning to cognitive activities. Although the responsibility for learning rests primarily with the
bishop, this is not to suggest that it rests solely
with him. The bishop is the final point of authority
and as such serves as an image of the church. All
learning takes place in community. It is next to impossible for a student, regardless of his own dedica-
tion, to learn within a community which despises
learning. How much easier it is to prepare sermons
from the Greek text if all one's colleagues are doing
so, than to attempt such a foolhardy task if the sermons in other local churches are arising from a collected works of Spurgeon or Moody, a Barclay assemblage
of New Testament words, or one of the many heaps of
adages and anecdotes provided by the electronic media.

It is not surprising that Alfred should have
chosen this work for translation, nor that the question of Christian education should have been first on
his mind. He lived in a society which had crumbled
socio-politically and spiritually. As king, Alfred
organized the army against overwhelming odds, began a
navy, revised the legal system, instituted taxation,
in all, renewed the political life of his people.
Once society was stabilized, he took a more active concern for his people's spiritual welfare. We must not
interpret his "turn" within the framework of naive old-
fashioned Marxists or their pragmatic capitalist
brethren who hold, each in their own way, to the view
that "culture" is the superstructural icing on the
basic cake. For men of Alfred's day, spiritual life

is the highest form of culture (cultivation) and without it material culture is meaningless, in a sense, non-existent.

Alfred does not finally turn to spiritual culture after the wars because he had time, but because the bishops needed prodding. The spiritual authority who are his authorities, under whom he serves God, had not been fulfilling their vocations; and Alfred, like all ancient and medieval men, a lover and master of irony, reminds them of this. As king he has no authority to tell the bishop what to do. His only word of command is the third word of the preface, "orders" (*hátath*); the opening sentence reads literally "Alfred the king *orders* that greetings be sent to bishop Waerferth," but after this initial order he sets aside his royal perogative. What he wants to say is "Christian wisdom has died in England, learning is your responsibility. I have looked after my area, but my work is nonsense unless you look after yours." He cannot issue such commands, however, for by so doing he would be rejecting the very principle he wishes to protect. Earlier blessed times, he writes, depended on the kings obeying God *and his messengers*. Therefore he does not remind the bishop of the great wisdom which there once was in England, but he tells Waerferth that he, Alfred, has been recalling it in his own mind, indicating quietly that things have changed since he came to the throne. He cannot command the bishop, but he can "bid [you] to do as I believe you wish to do." If the bishop had so wished why did he not act earlier? Alfred gives him the benefit of busyness and a world that will not listen, and writes: "Free yourself from worldly matters as often as you can so that you may apply the wisdom that God has given you wherever you can." But before his preface is completed Alfred has taken away the bishop's excuse and points out that he, Alfred, has found time to translate a major book on the bishop's role and that he will put one in every cathedral. On each one he has placed an expensive clasp, and on the pretext of the book's and clasps's expense, for which he has paid, he "asks" that no one take the book away, except in the case of a bishop who may, possibly, wish to read and publish it. His ironic intention is also evident in the line we had reason to reflect on earlier: the canon was translated; therefore *it seems better* to me, if you think so, for us also to translate some books which are not needful." Perhaps the sentence could be paraphrased "Since you have not done your job, it seems better to me to step outside of the limits of my proper authority and start the work, than to leave it undone."

We are likely to find Alfred's irony comic or repulsive, perhaps both. In our society where straight talk is considered a virtue, the use of rhetoric to hide rather than reveal is considered at the best, prevarication, and at the worst, hypocrisy. But Alfred's was not a world in which every thought was considered proper in every place. He lived before the days of the logical positivists and the belief in neutral language; for him all language was rhetorical, i.e. persuasive, intended to work an end. Rhetoric, as Aristotle defined it, is the art of persuasion.[4] If used for a false end, its use was sin; if used for the greater glory of God, it participated in the Word itself for the redemption of the universe. For Alfred, the Roman rhetoricism's adage was true: there is no such thing as a perfect orator, unless he is also a good man.[5]

It would be too complex at this point to discuss in great detail the importance of rhetoric for theology in the patristic and medieval periods. But rhetoric's importance must not be neglected by anyone hoping to interpret texts of Christians who lived during these centuries, indeed Christians who wrote the New Testament.[6] In the seventeenth and eighteenth centuries, theology was discussed in a systematic methodology which owed its primary form to philosophy; in the nineteenth century theology was thought of in historical categories. The nineteenth century historical focus is still with us but is slowly being replaced by a theology which is shaped by the social sciences. It is, as a result, difficult for us to imagine a world, like the patristic and medieval one, which regularly viewed theology in rhetorical terms. All the great patristic theologians were "men of letters," not systematic philosophers or historians. All were concerned with the literary quality of the scriptural text and of their own compositions (the Cappadocian Fathers and Augustine are the best examples). When they thought theologically, it was in terms molded by a rhetoric-philosophy debate in which rhetoric included much which we now consider philosophy (e.g., ethics), and philosophy was written in persuasive style (e.g., Plato and Cicero).

I have raised the question of rhetoric here for two purposes. Firstly, Alfred uses an ironic rhetorical mode in his preface: he does not consider it prevarication or hypocrisy. He uses it so as best to persuade the bishop to fulfill his vocation. Today as religion moves into the highly rhetorical medium of television and there are even greater demands for local pastors to fulfill the functions of the Christian Television Network's salesmen, the need for a proper interpretation of rhetoric's relation to theology becomes ever more important. We may then find help in meeting the new rhetorical challenges by returning to an art considered outmoded since the eighteenth century. Such a return might aid us in a second way. The brittle dogmatic formulations of the last three centuries are losing their hold on modern man, and the dangerously heretical presuppositions of the social sciences need to be opposed in so far as they shape theology into their faith assumptions in progress and the total freedom of the individual. A rhetorical model can renew the dying and replace the false by redirecting our attention from true-false statements to the analogical function of the Scriptures and Fathers who are at the source of our spiritual lives and who worked for the most part in rhetorical categories.

One final matter related to the question of rhetoric must be raised, albeit briefly. Alfred wished to stimulate his bishop to action and did so in an ironic mode. There is much he could have said, but he said little and that little with hidden intent. His rhetorical choice had a theological parallel, the doctrine of reserve.[7] God did not make his will known to humankind in one initial act following the fall but revealed it piece by piece throughout history until the "fullness of time," when human beings were properly prepared to receive it. God's order is received in its proper order. Certain matters are held in reserve until the one to be instructed is ready to receive them. All things are received according to the mode of the receiver. An infant receives the Bible as paper, a child as story, a teenager as God's justice, a youth as truth and a wise person as beauty and goodness. To attempt to explain the fullness of the justice, truth, beauty, and goodness of the scriptures to the infant would be foolishness. We begin our educational endeavors by beginning where the one to be educated begins. We reserve certain questions which can be understood only at a later point. Some day we will know even as we are known. God in the fullness of his "economy" has reserved perfect knowledge from us. Our Christian education endeavors must be then, thought the ancients and medievals, patterned according to God's order, his economy. As moderns, we can understand such a program for learning mathematics or any other discipline. We learn the arithmetical rules before we tackle algebra, algebra before analytic geometry, etc. We are offended however by the suggestion that such a practice should be implemented in our "theological" education. To us such "reservations" raise echos of some cultic program, inconsistent with the Christian spirit. Our reaction may have its place in our modern age but we must remember that the principle of reserve in the educational process, in spite of its "anti-democratic," "free access to information" bias, is intended for use only within the infinitely expansive discipline, theology, that it presupposes activity within a divine order and that it is directed

to ever more serious growth in spirit. The doctrine of
reserve does not say "this is all you can have for the
present," but "there is yet more to receive." The
modern loss of this principle and a rejection of its
concomitant concern with the infinite order may be
more than anything else at the basis of a contemporary
Christianity whose members find themselves peculiarly
fixated at elementary theology and who are as a result open to every simplistic wind of doctrine. Lest
anyone fear that the doctrine of reserve (interestingly
first formulated by the great rhetoricians in Alexan-
dria) will serve ecclesiastical totalitarianism, it
is well to remind ourselves that for the medieval any
statement made under reserve about past formulations
of theology were made by men and women who knew that
they were ignorant of the greater part of God's economy,
yet to be revealed to future Christians.

3. The Problem of Authority

Alfred, as already noted, was caught in a crisis
of authority which he overcame on the surface with the
use of irony. He overcame it in a second and more
profound way, however, by submitting to Waerferth's
authority and at the same time directing the bishop to
the authority beyond both of them.

Every modern student of ancient and medieval
literature is troubled almost immediately by the
problem of authority. Medieval theologians in particular quote the authority of Scripture and tradition
without hesitation. But whereas for us authority is
defined within a political and institutional setting,
for the medievals the term held no connotations of
authoritarianism, or the limitation of personal political
freedom. For them authority was defined in its simple
etymological sense: the authority of a thing is that
thing's author or source. Thus, faced with a society
in need of immediate renovation and reformation,
Alfred returned to the society's sources. The
Anglo-Saxons, he knew, had become a Christian people

because of the interest taken in them by Pope Gregory
the Great, who in 597 sent Augustine of Canterbury to
Kent to begin the conversion. As a result, Alfred
chose from among the most "necessary works," two by
Gregory, *viz* his *Pastoral Care* treating the secular wing
of the church, bishops and priests, and his *Dialogues*
which discussed the significance of the monastic or
regular order. Together these works would introduce
the reader to the whole Christian education framework
as experienced among the Anglo-Saxons. To be certain
that the English could remember their full "history,"
Alfred went on to translate or have translated a history
of the Anglo-Saxons by the Venerable Bede, *A History of
the Church among the English Speaking Peoples*, and the
more universal history of the world by Orosius. It may
be that the translations of Augustine's *Soliloquies* and
Boethius' *Consolation of Philosophy* were only the first
in what was to be a series of translations of "great
books."

For Alfred and his medieval and ancient forefathers,
to understand the authorities, the sources, was to
understand oneself. We are what our sources are. It is
important to grasp clearly this concept of authority.
The term was not primarily a political term; it was not
a term used in regard to the relationship between
contemporary individuals, one of whom held power over
another, nor was it primarily concerned with the relationship between contemporary *individuals* as singular
entities. A society is greater than the sum of its parts.
A society comes before individuals and is greater than
them. Two individuals do not make up the meaning of a
marriage or family, but marriage gives meaning to the two
individuals entering it. The English language does not
exist because we all speak it, but we all exist as
English speakers because there is an English language.
The language preceded us and will live after us. Society,
like language, transcends and makes us what we are. Society, like language, is not a tool we use, but a pool in
which we swim. For the medievals society, community,
comes first, and individuals second, and like language,

it is always historical. It is a gift from the past.
The authorities are not then *in* a society but *of* a
society. The authorities are the sources or authors
which beget the social values and institutions as a
whole. Society flows out of its authority as a stream
from its source.

For Christian society there is but one authority:
the son of God, Jesus of Nazareth. All Christian
culture or cultivation has its source in him. As
Jesus was an incarnated historical creature it is consistent with God's plan (God is faithful) that the
authority of Christ should be perpetuated historically,
i.e. in books by the Apostles and their followers.

Alfred makes use of a fascinating image to explain
more clearly the nature of Christian history and its
perpetuation. He has those educators who lived before the Viking raids speak as follows:

> Our forefathers, who formerly held these
> places, loved wisdom, and through it they
> obtained wealth and left it to us. In this
> we can still see their tracks but we cannot
> follow them, and therefore we have lost both
> the wealth and the wisdom, because we
> would not bend with our minds to the track.

Alfred's image here is easier to understand, if we
understand "forefathers" as literal, i.e. "those who
have gone *before* us, ahead of us." Our contemporary
view of history would look as follows:

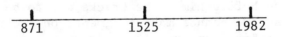

Alfred or the Anabaptists as our forefathers on this
chart are, in fact, *behind* us. Consider for a moment
Alfred's image of the *track*. The *Fore*fathers have
gone ahead into the wilderness and made a track which
will lead to the sea. The first of these was Christ:
he was the wedge (if I may so switch the image of the

cornerstone) breaking through the wilderness. After
him came others who followed his example, walking in
his track but continuing to cut forest on either side.
The picture of history which emerges is as follows:

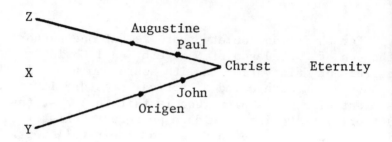

In this picture history is dynamic whereas in the
other history is static. To reach eternity one must
follow in Christ's track. But one must not negate the
significance of the word "follow." Following does not
mean walking happily and unconcerned with individual
"X." Rather, since Christ cleared forest, his followers to be truly followers clear forest and stand
with individuals "Y" and "Z." As a favorite theologian
of mine has written, "Theology mediates between a
cultural matrix and the significance and role of
religion in the matrix."

But how do we know where the track is? We must
"bend with our minds" Alfred tells us. The image is
clearly that of a scholar bending over his books, of
a student (the real meaning of the word "disciple" trans-
literated into English from the Latin translation
of the Greek) searching for wisdom by following those
who have gone before him. The tracks are to be found
in the books. We cannot make judgments on the track
by standing aside from it. If we do so we lose ourselves in the wilderness. Nor can we rest from following the track laid and continuing to widen it. If
we cease to do so, the wilderness will grow back in
and we may well lose the track altogether.

Consider Alfred's difficulty in light of this.
The track is to be found only in the historically
mediated written words of Scripture and the commen-
taries on Scripture available in the Fathers. The
role of Christian education was for him first and
foremost the importance of copying books. In a world
without print many precious thoughts could and were
lost. Where the path had once been widened brush grew
in and overcame it once more. For Alfred the task of
establishing monasteries and perpetuating learning was
the equivalent of saving the world from annihilation.
If the track was lost, all later people would be returned to the wilderness. "Consider what punishments
would come upon us *on account of this world* [future
peoples] if we neither loved [wisdom] ourselves nor
allowed other men to obtain it," he writes to Waerferth.
The first necessity of Christian education then is the
act of physically passing on the books of Scripture and
tradition in which the track lies clear to sight.

The act of passing on includes the interpretation
of the text, using the text as track while cutting
further into the wilderness. Paul, John, and Augustine
are as a result alive and with us today, our brothers
in Christ. In so far as we interpret them, they give
us direction for our time and insofar as they do that,
they grow by the interpretation. The writings of ancient authors are greater today than they were then.

Christian education must therefore always direct
believers to the authorities, the sources, if those
believers are to remain on the track. Again, it is
important to add that the believer cannot stand aside
from the track so as to judge it. There is no "place
to stand" outside of the track. The significance of
this can be made clearer by an example. There has
been much discussion recently regarding the historical
Jesus. Whether students in search of the historical
Jesus are pursuing him in the old search or the new
search, whether they are learned liberal clergymen or
ignorant conservative laymen (as a conservative and
layman myself, I feel free to so designate the latter),

whether they be attempting to pare off all extraneous
miracles or to get "back to the Bible," their problem
is the same. There is no return to a source outside
of the tradition initiated by that source and the
source with its tradition is therefore authoritative.
Again and again one hears discussion regarding the
historical person of Jesus. In such discussions, the
evaluations of Nicea and Chalcedon are set aside as
the erroneous attempt to explain the person of Jesus
by static Greek philosophic categories. What is forgotten is that the categories were not static. They
were not pigeon-holes into which the pure Jesus of
history was somehow stuffed. The categories of being,
substance, hypostasis, nature, and person were developed by the contestants to best explain their position. The terms come into our philosophical vocabulary
as they were developed in the midst of the christological controversies, not as they were developed before
them. In fact, to ask questions concerning the historical Jesus' "personality" is anachronistic since the
word "person" in particular developed in the fourth
century. Early Christians did not have an idea of person bequeathed them by the Greeks (Greek thought was
still troubled by the question as late as Plotinus)
which they then used to describe Christ; rather, they
worked out a concept of Christ's person and then, since
he was a man like them, used this concept to define
themselves. The notion of the unity and integrity
of the human person arises after Christians had come
to understand the unity and integrity of the two
natures of Christ, and reflection on that mystery
helped them to attain even greater insight into the
natures of their own persons until such reflection was
reduced to the mechanistic technological disciplines of the
modern epoch. The biblical text itself comes to us by
tradition and cannot be read aside from it. Punctua-
tion can be Athanasian or Arian: trilogues can be
simple three fold rhetoric or later trinitarian
shapings. We cannot get beyond history to the historical Jesus or beyond the tradition of textual transmission to the Bible itself. In western society this
is true for Christians and non-Christians. The problem

of existence and essence as faced by Sartre is a Christian problem reflected on in detail some eight centuries
earlier. Sartre is not so much a non-Christian as a
Christian positioned in the centre of the track and
walking away from the authority. It is the natural
problem of one who guides an automobile by the vision
projected in a rear-view mirror.

4. The Question of Tradition and the Role of Memory

For the middle ages the question of authority and
that of tradition overlap. To put our reading of
Alfred's text into a system which was only fully
developed 400 years after him, the matter of Christian
education is the authority, its effectors are the pastoral guides, its end as final course is wisdom (yet
to be discussed) and its form is tradition operative
in memory.

Tradition is bound to authority then as form to
matter, and as form it develops.[8] Tradition is a passing on of the authoritative sources by interpretation,
as we have already noted. When the authorities are
applied to new situations, i.e. when they are interpreted, they become greater than they were. It is
important to emphasize that there is a development of
doctrine in this interpretation but there is no progress. To paraphrase a nineteenth-century historian:
in theology we are all equidistant to eternity. We
are no closer to the "genuine" Paul today than were
our sixteenth century ancestors. Our technical knowledge of the Greek text may be better but the evidence
is against our better appropriation of his poem on
charity in 1 Corinthians.

Any mention of interpretation in the 1980s immediately calls to mind the modern hermeneutical
 problem.   But let us not suppose that the
 problem belongs solely to us. The middle ages and
their patristic forebearers were as well aware as
contemporary readers of Ricoeur and others that in
interpretation we take as much to the text as it brings
to us and that interpretation is never a simple matter.
In his Preface Alfred gives evidence that he under-

stands the problem. All interpretation is translation whether from a foreign language or from one's own, and it is affected by the "various and manifold troubles" of our material lives, by our choice to interpret "at times word by word, at times idea for idea" (the phrase is from Jerome writing on his translation of Scripture) by the extent of our intellect ("When I learnt it as I could best understand it") and above all by the community immediately around us (Plegmund and Asser, Grimbold and John [or Alfred]). All interpretation occurs within community. No Scripture is of private interpretation, as we are accustomed to hear, neither of the private interpretation, nor nineteenth-twentieth century historicists who cut themselves free of the tradition of interpretation. Nor of the private interpretation of individuals who cut themselves off from the humble helpfulness of their Christian associates.

There were many methods of interpretation in the middle ages but the most common was the four-fold method.[9] Sarcastically treated and severely attacked by Post-Reformation critics, it deserves review and rethinking for Christian educators in our own day. Patristic and medieval students of the Scriptures knew as well as their modern counterparts that any text is open to a manifold variety of interpretation This being so with secular texts, how much so must it be with the Sacred Text, it was believed, which should offer an infinity of interpretations. This they signified by the use of a *four*-fold method, not suggesting that all interpretations were to be straight-jacketed by these four, but pointing out that as four was the symbol of the natural world (four elements, four corners of the earth), a four-fold method was to indicate that within this world there would of necessity be an applied interpretation of Scripture for every student of the text at every moment of his or her life. The method began with the earth (literal level), moved to the mores (moral-legal dimension) of society (tropological level) and a consideration of a renewed society under the role initiated by Jesus of

Nazareth (allegorical level) and ended only in the
vision of new heavens and a new earth (anagogical level).
Each biblical text or story could be treated according
to all four levels. One begins with the obviously
literal meaning of the text, a meaning ascertainable
by using the methodologies of philology, poetics, rhetoric, historical-criticism, textual study, etc. One
can never avoid the literal or leap beyond it to other
levels. They are rooted in it just as we must find the
divine only in the physical man Jesus. On the literal
level we know that Adam ate the fruit offered by Eve
and that the word Adam symbolically relates him to the
earth as Eve relates her to the mother of all living.
The problem of the historicity of Genesis is not solved
by a literal reading. On the tropological level we
learn that people are at odds with one another, reduce
one another to evil and that will (Eve) leads reason
(Adam) astray. Allegorically we relate the Adam and
Eve story to the incarnate Christ. As Eve arose from
Adam's side so did the Church flow forth from the side
of Christ in blood and water (the sacraments). Ana-
gogically Adam and Eve's becoming one flesh is the
final union of Christ and his Church.

The dangers of the allegorical method are obvious.
By it one can read anything into the text one wishes to;
but as already pointed out, on the literal level as
well, one can read anything into the text. The literal
level includes the symbols of etymology and the results
of "literary" (rhetorical) reading. How does one protect oneself against such readings? The answer is simply "by attending to the text"--by practicing the art
of reading as medieval students practiced it. As
moderns, we approach texts to find out what is *in*
them, what message they will yield us if we apply the
correct literary, theological, philosophical or historical techniques. We separate ourselves from the
text by such techniques and with them force the texts
into their molds. For us the best reading is the
fastest reading with the greatest retention. We suppose that reflection on the content of a book will
occur after the content has been atained. Read and
make judgments, we say, but we offer no suggestions as
to how those judgments are to be made other than to ex-

pect that they will be made by the individual readers
separated from--at least following--a reading of the
book in question. A medieval reader approached a book
differently. Reading was oral, not silent, and oral
reading necessarily slows the reading speed as well as
aids the ability to understand. Even today we natural-
ly fall into an oral pattern when we come to a passage
which is too complex to understand on a first reading.
Reading was further slowed since the theological or
spiritual text was written in a second language, Latin.
The "foreign" and physically oral elements in the reading process meant that the text stood firmly as object
against the reading subject and could not be as simply
subjectivised as it can be in silent "speed" reading.
The medieval reader *attended* to the text, *waited upon*
it in reflection; for such a person all prayer began in
reading, reading gave rise to meditation or discursive
reflection on the words, and meditation to prayer and
contemplation. The medieval reader knew that he or she
was unlikely to understand a person if the person was
approached with suspicion: "Why did he say that? What
is he trying to get me to do? Does he have a father
complex? Is she an elder child? What stage of development has he reached?", etc. Such questions attain
their answers but not the person. We know persons
only as we are open to them. It is the same with texts.
Only in so far as the reader waits upon them, allows
them to speak back, will he or she ever truly read.
The reflection arising from *attending* or *waiting on*
the text is shaped by the text, not by the reader; and
as a result the reader becomes as it were, the book itself. The reader is shaped by the book, not influenced
by it. It is a case of becoming relevant to a text,
not requiring that the text be relevant to a contemporary situation. Only by such a reading method can the
grace of the authority, coming through tradition as a
free gift, ever be known.

The primary human operation which must be activated
in such reading is not the reason but the memory. The
medieval reader read slowly enough and reflected clear-

ly enough that the lengthy oral process allowed him or her to memorize the text as the reading proceeded.[10] Memorizing a book was the act of learning. It ought not then to surprise us that Bonaventure in the thirteenth century expected that one ought not to call oneself a theologian unless one has memorized the complete text of Scripture (how such a requirement might improve the theological morass of our contemporary society can only be imagined!).

Memory is the process by which the tradition is preserved. Alfred uses the word "remember" over and over again in his preface so as to emphasize this fact. First he tells us he "learns" the book from Plegmund and Asser, Grimbold and John (his congregation). And when he had learnt it (committed it to memory) "as [he] could best understand it and as [he] could most easily interpret it [the discursive reflection and mediation of it], [he] translated it into English [i.e. he transmitted the tradition]." Remembering the tradition is re-membering it, it is not simple rote memory. Remembering an authoritative text is putting it together again. Time moves on and members of a political social world change. The tradition must as a result be re-membered, integrated into the new setting.

This remembering is important for the health of society. As I sit at my table at this moment I *am* only in so far as I *remember*. In my hand there is a pencil. I hold the pencil and use it only in so far as I remember how to do so, that is in so far as I remember the day my parents taught me to hold the pencil. As I sit I am remembering a mechanical operation I learned at four months. As I hold my pencil I am a six-year old, and as I sit I am a six-month old. As I hear a speaker or read I do so accurately only in so far as I remember the meaning of the words, words I learned in the past. If I forget some part of my past I become a crippled person unable to act. If I forgot how to sit or eat, I could participate in no human activities.

Broken memories are broken people. The prime virtue is therefore not sincerity (as we moderns have it) but integrity. I am and am well only in so far and to the degree that I am and have well-integrated memories. Had I forgotten the past thirty years of my life I might be as sincere in my present occupation as I might be, but I would not be a moral, political, or religious person. It is the same with society. A society is integrated only in so far as its memory of itself is integrated, as its tradition is appreciated. Because of this Alfred worked so anxiously to translate and make known the sources of his world. The authorities of the society must be remembered so that the past as well as the present can be integrated.

To this point I have discussed the integral purpose of memory and that in a cursory fashion. Much remains to be said regarding its operation and function. Our contemporaries are accustomed to prefer thought to memory and to reduce thought, thinking, to the activity of the intellect or the reason. Intellect and reason they consider one and the same. Not so Alfred. He had learned from Augustine and Gregory that the source of human behavior is the memory out of which arise, while existing co-equally with it, the intellect and the will. Human beings are made in the image of God. God is a trinity. Therefore each person is a trinity. Our intellect is begotten from our memory as the Son is from the Father and the will is the mutual activity proceeding from them just as the Spirit precedes from the Father and the Son. Both intellect and will have their beginnings in the memory and are dependent on it. All our speculation arises from the intellect and all our practical decisions from the will. The memory is the source of both speculative and practical theology; it is not limited to *mere* learning or booklearning. The adage which distinguishes book-learned Christians from those taught by God (*Schriftsgelehrten, Gottesgelehrten*) is not an early medieval adage. Alfred could not have understood it. Nor is intellectual activity rational activity. We would do better to define the intellect by the word, understanding. As Thomas Aquinas

ould later make clear in his development of the
Aristotelian model, the reason (ratio) functions
discursively; the intellect or understanding *appre-
ends* reality.[11]

We must not define the concern with learning seen
in Alfred or other patristic and medieval writers as
sterile bookishness or cold soulless, loveless rational-
ity. Far too often books written by patristic and
medieval authors are described as works of dogmatic
theology when in fact they are prayerbooks. Anselm's
Proslogion, read today in philosophy classes and uni-
versities and therefore ignored as "too difficult for
the laity" by our congregations, is in fact a book
written for meditation. Reading it, waiting on its
words, reflecting on its words, remembering it, the
reader is to come to an experience of the greatness of
God, to be "drawn out" into eternity and to pray in
joyous knowledge and act. What we consider sterile
systematic theology and nit-picking, was for patristic
and medieval authors the soul of practicality.

"Why the senseless argumentation between the Athana-
sians and Arians over the relationship between the
Father and the Son?" shouts modern man. "What difference,
if they are of 'like' or of 'the same' substance?" For
patristic writers the difference had practical conse-
quences. The Father and the Son are one. If that
oneness was defined by subordinating the Son to the
Father, then there was danger that wives would in the
one flesh of marriage be subordinated to husbands
(even so "sexually deranged" a "male chauvinist" as
Origin insisted that such subordination was wrong),
that laity would be subordinated to clergy in the *one*
church, and that our redemption would be naught since
the believer who is of one faith, one baptism, and one
spirit with the Son would live a new life subordinate
and not of the *same* substance as the new life of the
Son.[12] Thus as systematic theology had practical effects
because of the analogical function of its parts, so too

the mysteries elucidated by it could become the best of
all meditative "texts" leading on to prayer and contemplation.

The relationship between the intellect and the
will, between speculation and practice is paralleled by
the relationship between the contemplative and the active lives. For a medieval Christian contemplation was
always primary. It was the center around which action
circled. A person is integrated only in so far as he
or she remembers and from the memory begets understanding. The action of the will arises thereafter. Without the former there is no activity. Likewise a society is integrated only in so far as its contemplative
operations are strong. For that reason Alfred was particularly concerned with the reestablishment of monasteries where men and women could be given the fullest
opportunity to read (remember), meditate (understand),
and pray (act). "By the prayers of the monks the
world is saved moment by moment from its inevitable
doom." When the bells call the monks to prayer, all
men pray. Around the monastery the universe circles,
at times not knowing its center. Prayer, we do well to
remember, is often defined by Paul as "making memory."

But Alfred did not limit this contemplative activity to the reading and writing-copying (they are really
the *same* activity) of the monks. He and the world
immediately before him and after him was unashamedly
"bookish," learned," and concerned with "schooling."
We will have time in a moment to reflect on the problem of illiteracy in the middle ages. For the present we must reflect on one further aspect of the
nature of learning. What has been said to this point
seems to suggest that the tradition to be remembered
is "purely" Christian, "fully" within the Church, and
takes no thought for political reality. I cannot
treat each of these problems in detail in this paper,
but their solution can be briefly outlined. A major
part of the tradition which Alfred, the patristic
writers, and later medieval scholars attempted to pre-

serve was that of pagan Greece and Rome. I have already commented briefly on this problem by noting that
much that we consider the peculiar possession of classical pagan culture, as in the case of philosophic terms
such as person, nature, substance, being, etc., is in
fact the result of Christian thought. We make too much
of a Christian-Classical division. The Tertullians who
shouted against pagan learning did so in the finest
Latin rhetorical style. Christians, as their Israelite
forefathers, collected the Egyptian wealth and with it
adorned the temples of a new creation. Almost all our
knowledge of Greece and Rome comes to us not aside from
the Christian tradition but through it. It was the
prayful copying of monks that preserved Horace and (yes)
Ovid. Cicero and Virgil, Plato and Aristotle are as
Christian as Isaiah and Ben Sirach. The creation, albeit fallen, is good and, directed to its proper end,
is magnificent. It is in this context that one may re-
consider the so-called Constantinian "fall." Alfred
continues the Constantinian traditions and his defer-
ence. To preserve the tradition, to integrate the
society as past and present, to re-member it, the
activity of both the religious and secular wings of the
society was and is necessary. The word is remembered
in learning, the spirit integrated in lives, the whole
incarnated in a new society. To suppose the possibility of a "pure" church aside from its incarnated activity in a real human world was for Alfred and his contemporaries, worse than heresy; it was a rejection of
the central mystery of the church, God become man. We
must always be on our guard then in remembering the
Constantinian era that we do not use some later technique such as the supposition of a "fall" or of a
radical division of an earlier pure church from a
later corrupt church to describe it. Only if we attend
to its words will it speak to us. The Scriptures and
the tradition in which they are received can proclaim
glad tidings only if the hearers' voices are stilled.

5. Wisdom and the End of Learning

The discussion to this point has seemingly been
limited to the schools of medieval society, and to the
learned, but the vast majority of people in Alfred's
day were illiterate. What of these people; how can
the educational ideal outlined above be related to
them? Asked from the point of view of Alfred's day it
poses few difficulties in answering. Asked from the
point of view of modern man, difficulties initially
seem insurmountable and cannot be overcome without a
serious attention (if I may now use the word in the
sense adopted above) to the image of ourselves reflected by Alfred's situation.

Alfred came to the throne at a time in which the
vast majority of his people were illiterate. The word
"illiterate"was not in his vocabulary and, as we understand it, it was not a problem for him. Certainly
he realized that there were fewer people who could
read Latin than there had once been and that there was
a real danger of this knowledge dying completely, but
his program of establishing schools and translating
the authorities was not an attempt to raise the level
of general literacy. Never in the history of the
world, as Alfred knew it, could all people read. The
possibility of general literacy as we understand the
term was unimagineable to him. His program of translation was not an attempt to bring all the books to
all the people.

As in Greece and Rome, long before Constantine, so
in Anglo Saxon England, the problem was not teaching
letters but producing books. It took one monk one
year to copy one Bible. Even with enough copyists
there was not parchment enough for a Bible in every
plow-boy's hand. In addition, the linguistic change
occurring in Latin and the vernacular languages between the fourth and the twelfth centuries was occurring at tremendous speed. Translations of any book
for general readership would have been physically im-

possible, even setting aside the need to feed, house, and clothe people experiencing rapid social change. Moreover, as all people of common sense know, every translation is an interpretation as is every reading, but a translation fixes a particular interpretation at a particular time. Translations of the Bible, in their text and words are not carefully scrutinized, have a way of "fixating" spirituality in a particular age. Better to remain with the original language (I am prepared to argue for the Vulgate as in a real sense "original," authoritative, for the west) and thus to follow primitive Christianity, than to find oneself held captive by the fourth or perhaps the sixteenth century. Better to do so, indeed, so as better to remember, so as not to read oneself into the text.

Alfred's work of translation must be understood in light of these comments. Although the Scriptures were translated (some indeed "in part" into languages other than Latin), he does not suggest that the Scriptures be translated; they were far too important to tamper with. He chooses to translate other works and he does so as a *first stage* in reestablishing Latin learning. The translations are to help one to read the original, to stimulate interest in the original. "The more wisdom there will be, the more languages are known." The best students born of free men are to move to a knowledge of Latin, Latin once fell into decay; and if it does so again, there will be translations which will help us return to it. The translation is for those who know "but little Latin." Ponies are acceptable in the learning of an ancient language.

Yet what of those youth not of free men, or those who are so born who do not have the time? Are they cut off from the integrated memory of the tradition and from the joyous prayer arising from it? By no means! This would only be the case if learning were rooted in the intellect and not in the memory, if the activity of memory were focused on "silent reading"

and not on "oral hearing," and if learning were an end
in itself. Medieval reading was always oral and was
not thus reading in our sense but *hearing*. Such reading (hearing) involved memory. Understanding arose
from remembered words, not from encyclopaedic facts
available only to those with the book or the computer.
Those who were unlettered were those without books
but not those without memories. Almost any medieval
sermon collection will convince the attentive reader
that the average person to whom such sermons were delivered must have had as great a knowledge of the
Bible and perhaps greater theological sophistication
than the average church goer in North America today.
Both laymen and clerics read daily the art, architecture, pictures, statues, sacred objects, morality and
mystery plays, liturgy, creeds, prayers, festal
seasons, etc. and above all the remembered meditations
on the relationships between the seven deadly sins,
overcome by the seven virtues which were in turn aided
by the seven gifts of the Holy Spirit, the seven sacraments, the seven petitions of the Lord's prayer leading
to a life in fulfillment of the seven(!) beatitudes.

The unbooked, the unlettered, could be as learned
as the lettered. The source of the learning of both
was the memory and for neither was learning an end.
The end of learning, as Alfred makes clear in a number
of places in his preface, is wisdom. Wisdom, for Alfred, is not set against learning but based on it.
The wise person is the person who having memorized
facts is able to apply them to a particular situation.
Wisdom is the proper application of what has been
learned. Memory remembers (i.e. recalls the past--
note the meditative function of recollection) and what
it learns it re-members as wisdom in the world presented to it. The worst possible sin for a learned
person is to make learning an end in itself. By the
thirteenth century this sin was defined by the term
curiositas (curiosity) learning for its own sake.
Theologically it was the equivalent of rejecting the
third member of the trinity, and sinning against the
Holy Spirit.

Whether lettered or unlettered, a Christian was to
earn in faith. "Faith seeking understanding" was not
n adage for the university alone. It applied to
very level of society. The wise interpreted (trans-
ated) the authorities to the present as did Alfred.
he wise were like Gregory, "versed in many doctrines
hrough the wisdom of his mind, his hoard of [actively]
nowing thoughts." And the wise who attained full
isdom could not appropriate the wisdom gained as their
wn wisdom; for having so reached the pinnacle of their
ife of faith, they understood that the word of wisdom
poken by them to a needy world was not theirs but
he same authority they received as a gift in memory.

. Continuations: Theology, Education and Reformation

The underlying principles of education held by
lfred and open to view in his preface remained firm
hroughout the middle ages. In fact one can still see
hem operative, although in another setting, in the
rotestant Reformation. One thing that is obvious
rom our reading of Alfred is that for Christians of
is day (and certainly for his Christian forefathers)
heological education was not limited to a select
schooled" few nor was it separate from schooling in
he faith, or spiritual formation. Learning was not
o be an end in itself but was itself to end by
rowing into wisdom and the love of wisdom (*philoso-
hia*). The greatest philosopher of the middle ages,
homas Aquinas (d. 1274) was in full agreement. His
onumental *Summa Theologia* is not, as it is so often
escribed, a systematic study of theology the purpose
f which is to arrive at *true* theology. Nor is it
ntended primarily for post-graduate students as op-
osed to those who are beginners in the faith. It is
ritten as Thomas himself says in the prologue to
ass on in the tradition (*tradere*) those things which
ertain to the Christian religion (*religio*), as is
itting for the erudition of beginners." Like Alfred,
homas is concerned with passing on the authoritative
radition. He too knows the role of memory. What

must be noted is that he deals with those things which pertain to the Christian *religion*. *Religio*, for Thomas, is a technical term. *Religio* imports (brings from abroad) the order or direction to God to which man is ordered. It is a virtue returning the honor which is owed to God and is preferable to all the other virtues. It is the statement of faith, hope and charity by which man is primord·aly ordered toward God.

Religio is tied closely to theology, it is the intention of theology. But we are not speaking here of theology as a speculative science. Theology, Thomas tells us, is wisdom, and its end is eternal beatitude.[13] The sum of theology (*Summa theologiae*) is directed to the beginners to lead them to this beatitude. This wisdom is ultimately Christ: its primary purpose is not to train Ph.D.s in the complexities of epistemology, but to draw out all the rude and lowly (*e-rudire*) into a greater sense of the greatness of God in Christ. And perhaps that is why at a deeper level the *Summa Theologia* was never completed--not because Thomas could or would not, but because, as it stands in its truncated form, it warns all that the memory, intellect, and will of each human person will never cease to reach out into wisdom. Each, an infant in Christ, begins with the milk of Thomas' words (in the first sentence of his work he quotes 1 Cor. 3:1-2), not with the meat of full faith, hope and love.

Thomas stands with Augustine, Gregory, Alfred and Bernard of Clairvaux against empty theological cogitation. Better to pray than to dispute (*orando quam disputando*) to be a theologian. "Faith seeking understanding" is not the act of the reason nor does it describe an "intellectual" act in our sense of the word. It is a *religious* act and as such, an act of devotion. Thomas understands the word devotion in its ancient sense of loyalty to a person, the desire to imitate and follow that person, to serve. It is close in its meaning to piety. Devotion for him is an act of the virtue of religion and subordinates man to God. The religious intellect prays, the religious will is devout, the religious body bows in adoration.[14] Prayerful faith devoutly seeks to adore in understanding wisdom. This is the task of each person, monk or priest, lay or cleric, booked or unbooked, sophisticated or "rude," literate or illiterate; it is the task of each person who piously seeks wisdom, the wisdom of the Authority, Christ as remembered in Scripture and tradition.

It is with great hesitation that I conclude this paper with a few comments on the Protestant Reformation, an area in which I am not a specialist and of which, with the exception of one unknown figure (Caspar Schwenckfeld von Ossig), know little. It will not surprise you to note that Schwenckfeld speaks often of the *School of Christ* in which all believers are learners (*discipuli*).[15] The temptation to speak at length on Schwenckfeld is great, but I choose for the present to deal with a far more significant figure, John Calvin. I am embarrassed to admit that I have begun to read Calvin carefully only very recently and that I have done so because my daughters began to attend a school operated by Dutch Calvinists. It was my eldest daughter's continual reference to the "cultural mandate" (the Calvinist equivalent of Mennonite discipleship?) that drove me back to a far too dusty copy of the *Institutes*. As I first turned to Calvin's major work, I expected to enter the sterile wastelands of the systematician; I expected this because I had been told that Calvin and his followers were somehow disembodied minds, stern, moralistic, unyielding, logical machines. One can imagine my surprise that when turning from the warm wonders of Thomas to Calvin's French 1560 preface I found myself in very familiar territory. It was like coming to Elkhart and finding Canadian students to talk to. The first paragraph of the 1560 preface is a near paraphrase of Thomas' prologue to the *Summa*. I am not suggesting at this point that Calvin knew Thomas (although it would not surprise me if he did and if he knew him well); I am suggesting that they both wrote within the

same tradition of theology. Thomas' *Summa* begins with
a discussion of sacred doctrine as reflected in the
Scriptures. Calvin speaks of the "perfect doctrine"
contained in Holy Scripture. Calvin speaks of his
readers as *bending* their intention "while reading the
work." In Scripture, he writes, are the "infinite
treasures of [the Lord's] wisdom." His *Institutes* are
for those who have "not much practice in it" for
"simple folk" (Thomas' "beginners") "in order to guide
them [*erudire*] to help them to find the *sum* of what
God meant to teach us in his Word." He will treat, he
says, "Christian philosophy," love of wisdom. The preface to King Francis fits Calvin even more closely into the patristic and medieval pattern we have been
discussing, "My purpose was solely to transmit [*tradere*?]
certain rudiments [sources?] by which those who are
touched by any *zeal* of *religion* [!] might be shaped to
true godliness [piety]."[16] Calvin's end, like Thomas'
is not "knowledge" in our modern sense but understanding leading to wisdom. In fact he begins his work
proper by speaking of wisdom and by drawing attention
to the contemplation of God. It comes as little surprise to read the opening sentence of the seventeenth
century author, William Ames, who read Calvin closely:
"Theology is the *doctrine* of living to God."[17] Doctrine
for us is now understood as an empty teaching, a meaningless piece of schooling to be learned only for the
sake of learning, as an end in itself. We tell children that Christians believe in the Trinity and that
they must believe it; and we believe that by doing so
we are teaching them and they are learning. When we
do so, we make learning an end in itself, and when
they reject it as a mass of sterile, meaningless formu-
lae, we lament the end of learning, forgetting what
our patristic, medieval and, perhaps Reformation forefathers knew: that learning is in fact to end, but to
end in the infinite dimensions of wisdom. We might do
well to return to the authority of their tradition;
the challenge will be in our re-membering it.

Alfred's Preface to the Pastoral Care

King Alfred sends greetings to bishop Waerferth
ith loving and friendly words; and I let it be known
o you that it has very often come into my mind, what
ise men there formerly were throughout England, both
f sacred and secular orders, and how blessed times
here were then throughout England; and how the kings
ho had power over the people obeyed God and his mes-
engers; and how they preserved peace, morality, and
rder at home, and at the same time enlarged their
erritory abroad; and how they prospered both with war
nd with wisdom; and also the sacred orders, how zeal-
us they were both in teaching and learning, and in all
he services they owed to God; and how foreigners came
o this land in search of wisdom and instruction, and
ow we now have to get them from abroad if we are to
ave them. So general was wisdom's decay in England
hat there were very few on this side of the Humber
ho could understand their divine office in English,
r translate a letter from Latin into English; and I
elieve that there were not many beyond the Humber [who
ould do so]. There were so few of them that I cannot
emember a single one south of the Thames [who could
o so] when I came to the throne. Thanks be to God
lmighty that we now have any supply of teachers. And
herefore I bid you to do as I believe you wish to do,
o free yourself from worldly matters as often as you
an, so that you may apply the wisdom which God has
iven you wherever you can. Consider what punishments
ould come upon us on account of this world, if we
either loved it [wisdom] ourselves nor allowed other
en to obtain it: we have only the name of Christian,
nd very few of the virtues. When I considered all
his I remembered also how I saw, before it had been
ll ravaged and burnt, how the churches throughout the

whole of England stood filled with treasures and books, and there was also a great multitude of God's servants, but they had very little knowledge of the books, for they could not understand anything of them, because they were not written in their own language. Thus they spoke: "Our forefathers, who formerly held these places, loved wisdom, and through it they obtained wealth and left it to us. In this we can still see their tracks, but we cannot follow them, and therefore we have lost both the wealth and the wisdom, because we would not bend with our mind to the track." When I remembered all this, I marvelled greatly that the good, wise men who were formerly all over England, and had perfectly learnt all the books, did not wish to translate them into their own language. But I immediately answered myself and said: "They did not think that men would ever be so careless, and that learning would so fall away; by their will they abstained from it [translation], and they wished that the wisdom in this land might increase with our knowledge of languages. Then I remembered how the law was first known in Hebrew, and again, when the Greeks had learnt it, they translated the whole of it into their own language, and all other books besides. And again the Romans, when they had learnt it, they translated the whole of it through learned interpreters into their own language. And also all other Christian peoples translated a part of it into their own language. Therefore it seems better to me, if you think so, for us also to translate some books which are most needful for all men to know into the language which we can all understand, and for you to do as we very easily can if we have tranquillity enough, that is that all the youth of free men now in England, who are rich enough to be able to devote themselves to it, be set to learn as long as they are not fit for any other occupation, until that they are well able to read English writing: and let those be afterwards taught more in the Latin language who are to continue learning and be promoted to a higher rank. When I remembered how the knowledge of Latin had formerly decayed throughout England, and yet many could read

nglish writing, I began, among other various and mani-
old troubles of this kingdom, to translate into Eng-
ish the book which is called in Latin *Pastoralis*, and
n English *Shepherd's Books*, sometimes word by word
nd sometimes idea for idea, as I had learnt it from
legmund my archbishop, and Asser my bishop, and
rimbold my mass-priest, and John my mass-priest. And
hen I had learnt it as I could best understand it,
nd as I could most clearly interpret it, I translated
t into English; and I will send a copy to every bish-
pric in my kingdom, and on each there is a clasp
orth fifty mancus. And I ask in God's name that no
an take the clasp from the book or the book from the
inister: it is uncertain how long there may be such
earned bishops; as now thanks be to God, there are
early everywhere; therefore I wish them always to re-
ain in their place, unless the bishop wish to take
hem with him, or they be lent out anywhere, or any
ne make a copy from them.

This message Augustine over the salt sea brought
rom the south to the islanders, as the Lord's cham-
ion had formerly decreed it, the pope of Rome. The
ise Gregorius was versed in many true doctrines
hrough the wisdom of his mind, his hoard of knowing
houghts. For he won over most of mankind to the
uardian of heaven, best of Romans, wisest of men,
ost gloriously famous. Afterwards king Alfred trans-
ated every word of me into English, and sent me to
is scribes south and north; ordered more such to be
rought to him after the example, that he might send
hem to his bishops, for some of them needed it, who
now but little Latin.

FOOTNOTES

[1] For a useful background to the topic see Henri Marrou, *A History of Education in Antiquity*, trans. by George Lamb (New York, 1956). Note as well, Pierre Riché, *Education and Culture in the Barbarian West*, trans. by J.J. Contrini (New York, 1976) for an excellent survey of the period discussed specifically in this paper.

[2] On Alfred see Eleanor Shipley Duckett, *Alfred the Great* (Chicago, 1956). For more extensive background on the period see Peter Hunter Blair, *An Introduction to Anglo-Saxon England* (Cambridge, 1959). The appended translation is from the Anglo-Saxon text as edited in *Sweet's Anglo-Saxon Reader*, revised by Dorothy Whitelock (Oxford, 1967).

[3] On Gregory the Great see F. Homes Dudden, *Gregory the Great*, (New York, 1905). For a translation of Gregory's *Pastoral Care*, see that by Henry Davis in *Ancient Christian Writers, II* (New York, 1978).

[4] Aristotle, *Rhetorica* in W.D. Ross (ed.) *The Works of Aristotle*, (Oxford, 1946ff), 1345^a.

[5] Quintillian, *Institutio Oratoria*, trans. by H.E. Butler (London, 1920), II, 9.

[6] The bibliography on ancient rhetoric and modern rhetorical theory is extensive. Note Donald L. Clark, *Rhetoric in Greco-Roman Education* (New York, 1959) and George Kennedy, *The Art of Persuasion in Greece* (Princeton, 1972) and above all, James J. Murphy, *Rhetoric in the Middle Ages* (Berkeley, Calif., 1974).

[7]For a brief history see Robin C. Selby, *The Prin-iple of Reserve in the Writings of John Henry Cardinal Newman* (Oxford, 1975).

[8]On tradition see above all Yves M.-J. Congar, *Tradition and Traditions*, trans. by Michael Naseby and Thomas Rainborough (London, 1966) and Josef Rupert Geisel-mann, *The Meaning of Tradition*, trans. by W.J. O'Hara (New York, 1966).

[9]The fullest discussion of this method is Henri de Lubac, *Exégèse médiévale*, 4 vol.; (Paris, 1959-1964).

[10]On memory see above all Frances A. Yates, *The Art of Memory* (Chicago, 1966).

[11]For an interesting modern commentary on this matter see Joseph Pieper, *Leisure* (New York, 1963), 28.

[12]See Origen, "Dialogue with Heraclides" in Henry Chadwick (ed.), *Alexandrian Christianity* (Philadelphia, 1954), 349ff.

[13]On *religio* see Thomas Aquinas, *Summa Theologica* 2—2 q.81 1; q94 1 ad 1; 2—2 q.101 3 ad 1. On theology see *ibid.*, 1q1 6; q1 3.4.5.

[14]*Ibid.*, 2—2 q.84.

[15]For a brief overview of Schenckfeld's thought see my *Schwenckfeld in his Reformation Setting* (Pennsburg, 1977) and the literature cited.

[16]See John Calvin, *Institutes of the Christian Religion*, trans. by Ford Lewis Battles (Philadelphia, 1960), I, 6-7, 9, 35-36.

[17]William Ames, *The Marrow of Theology*, trans. by John Dykstra Eusden (Boston, 1968), 77.

RESPONSES TO THE PAPER

James Schrag: I was hoping I would not be first. I can say that in relation to a line right out of the text: "Self-conscious about his own lack of education," Alfred did what he had to do about the low state of Christian education in his land. One of the aspects that interests me in this paper, which connects with my own situation, is the relationship between the king and his pastor bishop. I have a rather learned and influential layman in my church who is trying to get me to do something that he feels I ought to be doing. I'm starting with this because this may be the only place it will get raised in this whole seminar: the role of the pastor in Christian education. As an authority figure, Alfred had to be fairly directive in order to get his ideas about Christian education across. And although he was obviously much more capable of doing it than his pastor, he had given structures within which he had to work. I'm wondering, first off, whether we aren't in much the same situation today, like it or not. The pastor or bishop or whoever fills that authority role in the church plays a crucial part in the whole process of defining Christian education; and the pastors and bishops aren't always trained or predisposed for this task. We could think of various reasons why this is so. They didn't receive the proper kind of training in their seminaries, or they are over-burdened with other pastoral kinds of things. Already, I'm doing what a medieval person wouldn't do: I'm trying to psychoanalyze the relationship and I'm identifying first of all with the bishop, asking, "How do our pastors today receive that kind of admonition from laypersons who have a vision they haven't captured?"

Related to this, it was mentioned early in this paper that what is crucial is the kind of teacher who teaches, not what he teaches or how he teaches. If that indeed still has validity, all our various models and methods are placed on another level of importance in relation to the personhood of the teacher. I think that is something we generally acknowledge--that you can have the most marvelous curriculum and methods and audio-visuals, but it still only works if something is clicking in the person who's teaching. But what do we do to form this person and nurture the teacher?

Then, this paper makes a strong case, it seems to me, for studying church history as a part of the curriculum. If I understand all this business about our forefathers who have gone before and we are following in their tracks, that gives a very prominent place to our history, including memorization as a way of re-membering and assimilating the meaning of our history, and how we need to slow ourselves down by giving due attention to our past, and developing an attitude of reserve. Some of these things may be implied when we speak of the "teachable moment" in the Christian education process. Adults are at a different teachable moment in their understanding of Scripture and its meaning and application to their lives; and perhaps they are the ones who should be memorizing, not the children. If that is true, what part does memory work have for adults in Christian education?

Helen Reusser: I am used to being very honest, and my honesty is going to continue tonight. There is no way I can respond to Peter's paper. What's more I told him I wouldn't. I rode with him on the plane from Ontario. I met him at his home. He was putting his dog out for a walk--the dog he talked about-- and we had a good talk on the way down. I just don't feel capable of discussing what he put in his paper, and I'm not going to try.

I did pick up a couple of little things that I'm going to share with you. One is the importance of the teacher, which has already been mentioned. I've had many workshops with many teachers, and the thing that they say they get from the workshops is simply "a shot in the arm." I know how important it is to make the teachers feel important and feel that they can do the task and feel that they are the ones who are going to transmit the truth to the children. All the methods don't help at all if you don't have the proper teacher to transmit it.

careful about how strongly one attacks the so-called "schooling" model. I think I'll stop with that.

Winnie Swalm: As I listened to Prof. Erb tonight, I had a momentary fantasy: I thought perhaps if I could resurrect Alfred and bring him to a Brethren in Christ seminar on Christian education, it might be rather amusing to hear what he would say to us. If he can't make it, I'd be glad to have you come. I found your presentation really delightful. A number of things that came through to me have already been mentioned: the person of the teacher in Christian education, learning as a primary focus in pastoral care, the "fullness of time" principle in faith nurture, always with more yet to be known, and the doctrine of reserve. When we began this seminar this morning with the whole sweep of Biblical and historical experience before us, I was saying to myself, "Don't tell me we're going to start with the [invention of] the wheel again. Surely we've learned something already so that we can pick up at some point and go on with applications; but the emphasis tonight on returning to the source is so important, together with the image of the track; and then I thought that as we search for new frontiers in Christian education and try to formulate some new vision about the nurturing of faith, we best do this by returning to the source of the authority, the Son of God.

PLENARY DISCUSSION

Peter Erb: I have come to see that I misunderstood the intention of the seminar to some degree. I had thought there would be time for most of you to read the paper in advance, for obviously it's a paper to ponder and digest. I'd like to comment further on something picked up by Jim and Helen and Winnie: the question as to the kind of teacher called to teach. This came to focus in the development of patristic Christianity in the [debates about] the person of Christ. In fact, if you look at the development of patristic Greek, as well as Latin, you don't have the concept of person until the christological controversies. There's lots of scholarship I could send you to on the whole question of the role of the person in Greek and Latin thought. Our English word, "person," comes from the Latin word, persona, which is used in the way we use it for the first time when Christians tried to get a grasp of this person of Christ after Nicea and before Chalcida. And so in the Christian church, the first person who existed as persona in the western world--and one could make the case also for the Greek word, prosopa--is the person of Christ. When one talks then about the development of the persona of the teacher, the teacher is one who remembers and re-remembers Christ and who transmits the truth about Christ.

There's another comment I'd like to make about Jim's response concerning the role of the pastor. In this 9th century case study, the pastor-bishop was on the wrong side and had to be pressed a little to do what he was told to do. I have lots of concerns about seminary training in many traditions. I hesitate to speak about the Mennonite tradition because I don't know it in terms of seminary training, although I've been asked to reflect on this in the Seminary forum on Thursday. Perhaps the time has come for pastors to admit that there are some things they don't know, and that there are other people in the church who can fill the gap. I would not want my paper to be used to degrate the role of the pastor today, but just the opposite.

On your question of memory, I'd like to tell a simple little story. My brother and I were arguing like crazy one time about a particular topic--I don't even remember what it was; but it was in the presence of my grandfather, who said in the midst of our argument, "You know, what you're really talking about was kind of resolved by Tennyson." And then he quoted a little refrain from Tennyson's In Memoriam, which applied to the point we were arguing, bang-on. My brother looked at me and I looked at my brother because we expect nobody to read Tennyson until they get to third year honors English. My grandfather only got to grade six, and yet he could quote passages from Virgil in English, and he

And the other comment I picked up is that it's next to impossible to nurture the faith in a community that despises learning. Sometimes I worry about pockets of people in our churches who really seem to despise learning, and I wonder how in the world we are going to transmit learning when they're despising it.

Helmut Harder: I should be honest like that too, but I think I'll bluff my way through! Frankly, I would need a good deal more time to see whether anything significant might come from my reflections on this paper beyond what Peter has already clarified. I recall back in graduate school in Toronto wandering down to the lower precincts of the medieval library, where I met Peter Erb for the first time; and I was very impressed.

This is a gutsy paper. It's gutsy in the sense that he really sticks his foot out and kicks a lot of things around. It's an interesting paper; and it's a good evening! Peter has the advantage over most of us in that he knows medieval thinking, and I think few of the rest of us do, at least I don't. And so I believe him, whatever he says.

Regarding the medieval ages and regarding Alfred: he must have been a fantastic fellow. To think of statemen having that kind of insight; that's really rare. I wish Trudeau had a little more of it.

Many of the things in this paper I really believe in intuitively, I think. They undergird what I've stood for, even though I haven't articulated it. I don't want to go down the list too much, but I refer to the place of the text, the role of memory, tradition, hermeneutics—all these things ring a bell; and I think we've been personally deprived in the fact that we haven't paid more attention to that crucial period in history prior to the great breakthrough which we've enjoyed in the sixteenth century. In defense of the Foundation Series, I would want to say that I think we have tried in our faltering way to emphasize some of the items which Peter puts his finger on as being very important. The emphasis on historical theology intrigues me personally, a key I think to all we do to nurture the faith, a personal conviction that we need to come at Christian education again and perhaps more basically from the theological perspective, and that doing so will give us the key, the fulcrim for working at it. I don't want to put this over against the psychological principles of Christian education or the techniques of teaching, but rather in terms of what should come first. The question of passing on the books, the scriptures, the texts, Peter's statement that the first necessity of Christian education is the art, the act of physically passing something on—the books of Scripture. Continuity is so important. I wonder, however, if Alfred helped us that much with the problem of discontinuity. Psalm 78, for instance, tells adults to tell the great parables of the past to their children; but it's not only for the sake of memorizing them for or discerning the acts of disobedience. That psalm goes through a long recital of those times when Israel failed, and again and again God helped them. Kierkegaard was trying to tell us that (forgive him for being a modern) when he told us that sometimes we have to start all over again with our generation.

One last item on the first page of the paper—the point about the church being the umbrella for the medieval conception of Christian education, not the congregation, not the nation. I wonder if we shouldn't hear that. In reflecting somewhat on congregational life today as a basis for education, we may be a bit short-sighted if we don't recover some of the medieval perspective. Perhaps I am speaking somewhat defensively, because I work at Christian education in an institution that is not congregationally based, but which is more church based. At least it's a conference institution. And I think of myself as vitally related to the whole task of Christian education, including that part of it which happens within the local congregation. But the congregation is only one small unit of it; and I think in our modeling here in this seminar we should remember that there are institutions which override local congregations and which may be every bit as vital for the nurturing of the faith of our people as the so-called Sunday school; and I think too in this connection that one should be could quote passages from Aesop's *Fables*, and he could quote passages from Tennyson and MacCauley and Matthew Arnold. He didn't know who these men were. He'd learned them from his old school books; and as a child in grade school, he'd been taught to memorize these passages in such a way that had a particular application when his two sophisticated grandsons, each with their Ph.D.s, were arguing about some minute point in philosophy. He could put his finger right on the problem. Now that's really what I mean by memory, and it's necessary for children, and it's important for adults. And I do not mean memory by rote. There's a famous statement by Laurence Stern, made famous by that Penguin book called, *The Book of Turns*, on the important difference between memory and rote learning.

The last point I want to make, in response to Helmut's comment, is that those people in the 9th century did come to grips with failure. In fact, it is the story of failure. Alfred recalled a time when things were better, but they had forgotten, and they had to remember it again.

Leland Harder: My watch says nine o'clock, and I think we're going to adjourn very soon. But we'll still take any really urgent questions or comments.

Don Augsburger: The diagram on the blackboard keeps intriguing me, and I don't want to exegete out of it more than you have in it. The line from 664 AD to 871 AD is not 180° and it's not linear. What determines whatever curve you have there--75° or 80°? What determines the swath that Christian education has?

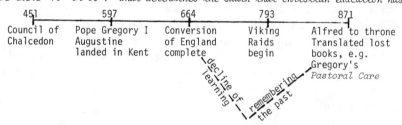

451	597	664	793	871
Council of Chalcedon	Pope Gregory I Augustine landed in Kent	Conversion of England complete	Viking Raids begin	Alfred to throne Translated lost books, e.g. Gregory's *Pastoral Care*

decline of learning / *remembering the past*

Peter Erb: It's interesting that you used the word, swath, because in Old English that's exactly the term that is used at one point. One thing we should observe for Alfred's day is that if you don't keep cutting, i.e., transmitting the books, the wilderness will grow back. It can grow back in one or two generations, and Alfred saw himself as someone in that century having to cut back again. What determines this? You can't answer that simply, but certainly what directs it is the Spirit of Christ moving through history. A characteristic of the middle ages I would observe with emphasis is a high sense of the Spirit of Christ working through history, a high theology of the Spirit.

C. J. Dyck: I'm sure that Peter and I could talk about these things for a long time yet. I appreciated the humor and the approach--a highly idealistic approach. It's a good antidote to what Mennonite historians usually do. We study the early church, the 16th century, and then move to our own era. Our bypassing those thousand years is epitomized by the venerable Baptist historian, Kenneth Scott Latourette, who entitled his volume on that period, *A Thousand Years of Uncertainty*. That's been our attitude, and I appreciate very much that you accented some of its positive contributions.

Leland Harder: Anticipating tomorrow's agenda, I can predict some more discontinuity as well as continuity with what we have covered today. We have sensed in this paper tonight a stance that, as Peter indicated in reply to Helmut, takes the lostness of a generation very seriously, but yet--with a kind of reserve until the people to be instructed are ready to receive the renewed revelation. Tomorrow, we will continue our search for a stance in Christian education that we can recommend to our churches. So get a good night's rest, and be here for worship at 8:30 o'clock.

ANABAPTIST-MENNONITE PERSPECTIVES

Cornelius J. Dyck

The focus of this paper is upon an analysis of how Anabaptists and Mennonites have transmitted, sustained, and nurtured faith. Doing this in brief format will need to assume a general knowledge of both Anabaptism and Mennonitism as well as of the other Reformation movements and their legacies. Anabaptism and Mennonitism must be seen in context. These movements have both borrowed from, and rejected, elements of other traditions from the sixteenth century to the present. Historically Mennonites have tended to lose their vision when they became culturally and geographically isolated. Some of the best things Mennonites affirm today they owe to others. What these things are may emerge as our study progresses.

Anabaptist and Mennonite writings on Christian nurture are extensive. The works of Menno Simons, Dirk Philips, Pilgram Marpeck, Peter Walpot and numerous other writers of the first generation contain many references. Those of succeeding generations are no exception, as the articles and bibliographies on education in *The Mennonite Encyclopedia* and elsewhere evidence. A number of articles may also be found in the *Mennonite Quarterly Review* (October, 1931) 231-241, (July, 1962), 243-255, (April, 1973) 102-114, and others. Noteworthy also is J. C. Wenger's *The Church Nurtures Faith* (1963), and Leland Harder's "The Concept of Discipleship in Christian Education," published in *Religious Education* (July-August, 1963) 347-358. In 1968 John A. Hostetler compiled a source collection of *Anabaptist Conceptions of Child Nurture and Schooling*. The papers of the Men-

nonite Church study on the *Philosophy of Christian Education* also became available in 1968, followed in 1971
by Daniel Hertzler's summary volume: *Mennonite Education: Why and How?* including a helpful bibliography.
I. E. Hartzler's *Education Among the Mennonites of America* (1925) also must be mentioned in this listing,
as must Gideon G. Yoder's *The Nurture and Evangelism of Children* (1959), and smaller, more recent pamphlets like
Cornelia Lehn's, *The Education and Conversion of Children,* which also includes a bibliography. This and other
uncited literature on the subject, however, is not so much an indication that all homework has been done as it
is a commentary on the necessity of continual study of the issue in the new and ever-changing cultural land-
scape of each generation.

Humanist and Medieval Roots

We can hardly think of Christian education without
thinking of the historical and continuing influence of
humanism. Both the secular Italian and more religious
Northern humanism of the fifteenth and sixteenth centuries helped to shape educational theory and practice as
we know it in the Western world today. The church has
rightly often feared humanism and, at times, opted instead for the path of indoctrination, but the Christian
educational task has thrived best when the created
order, including human nature with all its freedoms, com-
pulsions, and questions has been taken seriously. To do
this is particularly difficult in a sectarian or counter-
culture context.

The recovery of the classical languages was a particular gift of humanism to the church. This was epitomized in the 1516 Greek edition of the New Testament by
Erasmus (d. 1536). Men like Thomas More (d. 1535) and
John Colet (d. 1519) lectured on biblical texts even before they had studied theology. However, many of the
humanists were laymen. Their ridicule of church practices and abuses prepared the way for Luther, Zwingli,
and other more religiously inclined reformers.

Melanchthon, the "teacher of Germany," was undoubtedly the leading humanist educator. From 1524 until
his death in 1560, he worked tirelessly to establish
schools for clergy, lay people, and children. The educational system of Germany to this day, from university
to elementary levels, is generally considered to be
heavily indebted to his work. Under his direction,
school and church worked together to promote basic public education and what today would be called liberal
arts studies. The shape of Protestantism in Europe was
significantly influenced by Melanchthon's efforts and
educational philosophy.

Even more important, from a believers' church perspective, was the work of John Amos Comenius (d. 1670)
of the Moravian Brethren. His emphasis upon unity and
love among Christians, his conviction that education included the whole person and not simply the memorization
of abstract facts, and his primary objective as the development of Christian character need further study.

Early sixteenth century Anabaptism drew upon both
humanist and medieval roots for its understanding of
education, with the Swiss Brethren drawing more on the
former perhaps, and the Dutch Mennonites on the latter,
though Arnold Snyder's argument that Schleitheim was
heavily indebted to Benedictine monasticism must be
taken seriously. There is, for example, less emphasis
on conversion among the Swiss than among the Dutch
where both Menno and Dirk wrote treatises on the new
birth. We note, however, that in Grebel's 1524 letter
to Thomas Müntzer he writes in relation to baptism,
"that it signifies that a man is dead and ought to be
dead to sin and walks in newness of life and spirit,
and that he shall certainly be saved if, according to
this meaning, by inner baptism he lives his faith. . ."[1]
We also know Hubmaier's confession:

> Therefore I openly confess before God and all
> men, that I then became a Doctor and preached
> some years among you and elsewhere, and yet

had not known the way unto eternal life. Within two years has Christ for the first time come
into my heart to thrive. I have never dared to
preach him so boldly as now, by the grace of
God. I lament before God that I so long lay
ill of this sickness. I pray him truly for
pardon; I did this unwittingly, wherefore I
write this.[2]

The point at issue here, however, is not conversion
but the soil out of which early faith came. Menno and
Dirk had both received priestly training, but within
the context of the semi-ascetic Roman clerical tradition
and surrounded by the milieu of the Brethren of the
Common Life and Sacramentarianism. It is not surprising
then that their treatises on conversion reflect the em-
phases of these traditions on inwardness and subjectiv-
ity of faith in anticipation of later pietism which was
to have a strong influence on Mennonite faith and nurture in the nineteenth and twentieth centuries. The
linguistic and humanistically acquired hermeneutical
skills of Grebel and Mantz may have served a more original and creative function in small Bible study circles.
We cannot really see Grebel or Mantz saying "the Word
is plain and needs no interpretation," as Menno said,
though they would have agreed with his intended stress
on obedience as primary. We think also of Denck, for
example, whose humanistic training enabled him to translate the prophets.

The awareness that sixteenth century Anabaptism was
rooted in both the humanistic and medieval priestly-
monastic traditions helps to explain why they read the
Bible the way they did. The forthcoming *Reader in Anabaptist and Mennonite Hermeneutics* by Willard M.
Swartley, editor (1982) will serve a significant role in
helping us to understand their methodology. It may be
that Sattler's "How Scripture Should be Discerningly Ex-
posited"[3] is the most significant bridge document between
humanism and medieval motifs in Anabaptist hermeneutics.
There is no doubt about the fact that all Anabaptists

took the Scriptures seriously as the very Word of God.
This includes Denck and Marpeck in their struggle with
the inner and the outer Word. The humanist root did not
undercut the authority of the written Word, nor the
general Anabaptist emphasis that all Scripture centers
in Christ who, through the power of the Spirit, holds
the key to its right understanding.

The humanist and medieval motifs were a central ingredient of most Reformation developments. Why then
did Anabaptism differ so radically from the norms of
the Reformers? Because Anabaptism followed humanism in
its concern for moral reform, whereas Luther, while
equally concerned, was unable to break with the medieval
synthesis of Constantinianism and sacramentalism. This
moral concern led to the vision that the church in the
Bible might be restored in essence and form, becoming
again as it were, a first generation community. The
implications of this vision are enormous; the weight of
tradition is lifted, the Bible is affirmed as normative,
and each individual is called to responsible participation. All of life is seen as sacramental and holy.
Every doctrinal formulation is then made in this context
and the didactic task of the new community is not so
much one of transmitting the faith as it is living it
and testifying to it.

It is generally assumed that a discipleship ethic postulates a free will, which is essentially a correct reading of Anabaptist understandings, provided the function of grace is not eliminated. Grace affirms the sovereignty of God. While there were shades of difference among Anabaptists concerning the will, with Marpeck perhaps closest to Augustinianism, all believed a) that the individual has freedom to choose right from wrong, to affirm or deny Christ, and b) that divine omnipotence has determined the overall course of history to the end that the evil one will ultimately be destroyed and God's kingdom will come. God permits sin because he will coerce no one. Salvation is for all, but willful disobedience forfeits it unless repentance follows.

Is there then original sin? The Anabaptists seldom spoke to this issue, except when confronted with it in debate. They believed that there had been a definite fall from grace within history through disobedience. Therefore all persons are born as sinners *potentially*, but actually the tragic disobedience of the first Adam has been overcome in the full obedience of the Second Adam, Christ. Therefore, some asserted, it is actually better to be born after the fall than to have been in the Garden of Eden before the incarnation of Christ. Some, like Menno, believed that children were sinners but it was not counted to them as judgment until they of their own free will chose to disobey the divine calling. Many, however, were closer to Hubmaier who relied heavily on Ezekiel 18:20 "The soul that sins shall die. The son shall not suffer for the iniquity of the father, nor the father for the iniquity of the son." There were some tendencies to perfectionism in Anabaptism, particularly in the second generation, but not many.

Children: There are numerous references to the nurture of children in Anabaptist writings. In Grebel's 1524 letter to Thomas Müntzer he wrote: "We hold . . . that all children who have not yet come to discernment of the knowledge of good and evil . . . are surely saved by the suffering of Christ, the new Adam . . ." Similarly, in his confession of faith, Marpeck wrote: "Children have before the use of their reason no sin, for the proclivity to sin is the only thing they have and this does not harm their salvation until it actually breaks out into open sin . . ."

A study of Peter Walpot's *School Discipline* of 1578 confirms that the Hutterites saw discipline and growth in understanding as going hand in hand. Ulrich Stadler argued that children have no self-will and, therefore, no sin, but there are some traces of Hutterite feeling that the will of a child must be broken. Menno believed that children have the ability to choose when they achieve certain maturity and, with that maturity, a functioning conscience which also produces feelings of guilt and, hence, the need for forgiveness. In general Anabaptists saw children as important in their own right, not only because they would eventually be adults. Nevertheless, obedience and discipline remained central to nurture.

Conversion: In addition to understanding the role of children in Anabaptism as part of their affirmation of freedom of the will, the place and meaning of conversion is also central. While both Luther and Calvin refer to a particular spiritual experience in their life, the references are short and do not carry their theological understanding. In contrast to this the Anabaptist emphasis on the new birth is central to their thought, if not always articulated explicitly as mentioned earlier. The noun *metanoia* signified a change of heart and mind, it was part of the action of God in Jesus Christ in forming the new community. As in Acts 2:37, 38; 3:19, it was always coupled with repentance, turning back to God. Some described regeneration as the act of God making conversion possible through the working of his Spirit, and conversion as the human response. But regeneration may also be taken as the larger term, including both justification and sanctification. It is

not unfair to state that Luther's primary concern was
with justification, while the Anabaptist concern was
with sanctification; the latter would give evidence that
the former had taken place. This unity of conversion and
obedience is found in many writings, for example, in
Menno's comment: "In your life you must be so converted
and changed that you become new men in Christ, so that
Christ is in you and you are in Christ . . . 2 Cor. 5:17"
(*Works*, 96-97). Discipleship was seen as impossible
apart from the new birth. There was, however, no set
stereotyped expectation about how conversion should take
place, only that it must. This became an acute problem
with the second generation and later. Lutheran theology
has tended to argue that conversion belongs only in a
missionary situation, being replaced by nurture in a
Christian cultural setting.

Membership: Baptism and church membership are part
of this understanding of conversion and free will. The
usual emphasis in Anabaptist studies is to stress believers baptism as the requirement for membership.
This is taken as a kind of surrogate for the ability to
follow the Dominical injunctions of the Scriptures and
the admonitions of the community. An excellent text
combining grace and discipleship harmoniously is found
in Hubmaier:

> What must I know, or how much must I know, if
> I want to be baptized? The answer: this much
> you must know [of] the Word of God before you may
> be baptized: that you are a miserable sinner,
> and confess it, also, that you believe in the
> forgiveness of your sins through Christ Jesus,
> and you desire to begin a new life with the
> purpose of amending your life in conformity
> with the will of Christ in the power of God,
> Father, and Son, and the Holy Spirit. And you
> must know that if you go astray therein, you
> will, according to the rule of Christ in
> Matthew 18, permit yourself to be chastised,

whereby from day to day you may grow in faith
just as a mustard seed reaches the heavens.[4]

According to Menno (*Works*, p. 743) the meaning of
membership includes believing and teaching unadulterated
pure doctrine, using baptism and the Lord's Supper in a
Scriptural way, being obedient to the Word, brotherly
love, boldly confessing Christ, and a willingness to
suffer for him. The way of discipleship was also to be
followed in economic and personal affairs, including
nonconformity to worldly standards of conduct. Many
divisions came about in early and later Anabaptism-
Mennonitism because these criteria became a legal norm
enforced by the ban. When the dynamic power of the
Spirit had departed, a rigid traditionalism entered the
vacuum. Voluntarism was all but replaced by the pressures of conformity to the group. Baptism then no longer
symbolized new spiritual life and faith but a routinized
mechanism for the recruiting of members, not unlike that
practiced by infant baptizers.

Literary Resources

The Bible, including the Apocrypha, was the primary
document used for instruction and nurture among the Anabaptists, to which a growing volume of other writings
were gradually added. The literature of verification on
this is so abundant as to not need further elaboration
here. It should be noted, however, that some of the additional materials came quickly. We think of Hans Krüsis'
book on faith and baptism of 1525,[5] Sattler's treatise
on how to discern Scripture (1526) referred to earlier,
the hymns written by the prisoners in Passau in 1537,
later known as the *Ausbund*, which soon became a significant didactic instrument, the martyr collection *Het
Offer des Heeren* of 1562, the writings of the major
leaders, to wit: Hubmaier, Denck, Hut, Marpeck, Hoffman,
Menno, Dirk, Obbe, and many others. Early confessional
statements like Schleitheim, Hubmaier's instructions
about baptism and liturgy, the Dutch confessions and
martyr collections, as well as the 1582 hymnbook of Hans

de Ries served the same purpose. By 1600 dozens of books by and for Anabaptists were available, most of them in small format to facilitate easy concealment in baggy clothing. None of this material, however, took the place of the Scriptures and the personal admonition within the fellowship.

Much of the literature appearing after 1600 has been adequately chronicled by Robert Friedmann in his *Mennonite Piety Through the Centuries* (1949). Several items, however, require particular attention.

First among these is the devotional literature which arose in the Netherlands as an early type of pietist writing. We think particularly of Pieter Pietersz' *Way to the City of Peace* of 1625. It was widely read and published, and so anticipates John Bunyon's *Pilgrim's Progress* of 1678 that the question of influence arises. So also Johann Philip Schabalie's widely circulated *The Wandering Soul* of 1635 must be seen as a significant didactic instrument among and beyond Mennonites. A similar document used widely in the education of young people and adults, both in Europe and America was the *School of Moral Virtues* by Tieleman J. Van Braght, the compiler of the *Martyrs Mirror*. This appeared originally in 1657 and was still being reprinted in the nineteenth century.

A different kind of literature, today commonly referred to as a catechism, first appeared among the Dutch Mennonites in 1633. It was written by Peter Jansz. Twisck, the conservative, self-appointed successor of Menno Simons, at Hoorn. However, it was not prepared for the instruction of young people but of parents. It was his conviction that the education of children and young people was the primary responsibility of the home. Consequently his catechism was entitled *Instructions on How Parents and House Fathers Should Teach Their Children and Servants*. Additional catechisms were published by Reynier Wybrands, Hermanus Schijn, and others.

Nevertheless, by mid-eighteenth century many congregations in the Netherlands were offering catechetical instruction in church on Sunday afternoons. In part this was due to inadequate moral teaching in the home, but mostly because elders of the congregations felt new members to be ill-prepared doctrinally for membership. These catechism classes quickly also became inquirers classes for persons from other religious traditions, especially Calvinism. Other catechisms were produced according to local need. The one by Gerrit Roosen of Hamburg in 1702, and the Elbing catechism of 1778 continued to be very popular in Prussia, Russia, and America. Catechisms, however, were not used extensively by the Swiss or South German Mennonites until the eighteenth century. The Mennonite Brethren church eventually ceased using them because they sensed a conflict between it as a nurture device and the personal conversion which the Holy Spirit brings in the life of a seeker. The catechetical route seemed to make it too easy for "birthright Mennonites" to join the church without the necessary primary faith commitment.

Other Educational Institutions

The Mennonites in The Netherlands did not establish private schools except the seminary in 1735. A similar pattern prevailed, with several minor exceptions, in Germany, including Prussia. It was in Russia where the private school first became a fully developed part of Mennonite community life, due in large part to surrounding cultural and linguistic barriers. At first they were established and controlled exclusively by the church and considered an extension of its nurture program. The curriculum always included religious instruction. Later, under the influence of Johann Cornies (d. 1848), there was some "secularization" of school control by allowing colony administrative influence. By the time of the Bolshevik Revolution Mennonites had approximately four hundred fifty elementary schools in Russia, 25 secondary schools, two schools of business (commerce), four Bible schools, and two teacher-training institutes. Plans for the establishing of a seminary were aborted by the Revolution. The presence of these schools in every village and colony, and the fact that all Mennonite children and young people attended them, made it unnecessary for the congregation itself to engage in educational activity beyond the normal Sunday morning worship service. The elders did, however, carry out catechetical instruction annually prior to baptism. Today the vast Mennonite educational network which existed in Russia is gone, but its legacy can be seen in institutions in both South and North America.

In colonial America the family once again came into its own as the primary locus for education. Small elementary schools arose here and there to meet local needs. The best known of these was, of course, the one established by Christopher Dock on the Skippack about 1714, and again 1738. Dock's pedagogical principles are developed at some length in Gerald Studer's excellent biography as well as in J. E. Hartzler's *Education Among Mennonites of America* (1925). Dock's "One Hundred Christian Rules for Children" is well known. Of these rules 36 deal with one's relation to God, 28 with one's relation to the neighbor and 36 with one's relation towards oneself. It is likely that Dock's considerable gifts were strengthened through the influence of Comenius (d. 1670).

Nevertheless it was only in late nineteenth century that both the Russian and American (Swiss) Mennonites in North America entered seriously into the educational enterprise. On the part of the Russian Mennonites it was largely a continuation of what they had been used to in Russia, but among the American Mennonites the impetus came from a variety of socio-cultural factors, not least of which was the erosion of membership ranks through a loss of identity as a Mennonite people. Among the latter there was, and continues to be, a strong interest in church related elementary and secondary education as well as at college and seminary levels. While concentrating more on secondary and college as well as seminary education, the Mennonites from Russia showed particular interest also in Bible schools, especially in Canada. This interest was also shared by the American (Swiss) Mennonites. In earlier years the schools were called "winter Bible schools." Many have been discontinued. Others, however, have expanded their programs to include a total Bible school curriculum of two or three years, normally assuming high school graduation for matriculation.

With growing proliferation and curricular expansion, Mennonite schools seem to have loosened their ties to the church, though all of them count on the church for student and financial support and consider themselves accountable to their constituency. Inter-institutional and inter-Mennonite cooperation may have increased since World War II but the need for each institution to have its own unique identity remains strong. On the other hand there has been a great increase in efforts at defining the uniqueness of these institutions in relation to their culture and other similar institutions. A large percentage of the leadership in Mennonite conferences, congregations, and agencies comes from these denominational institutions. Whether these same people would have been available anyway is an untested question. There is no doubt, however, that most of these institutions have contributed significantly to the strengthening of Mennonite identity and purpose in the twentieth century.

Home Based Education

The sixteenth century conviction that Christian education must be centered in the home had not been lost in the transition to America. The primary promoter of education among Mennonites in America in the second half of the nineteenth and early twentieth centuries was John F. Funk. It was, in part at least, out of this concern that he began publishing the *Herald of Truth* in 1864. In the August 1866 issue he published the following ex-

cerpt from "Rules for Home Education," which he either
drew up himself, adapted, or simply borrowed from elsewhere:

> From your children's earliest infancy inculcate
> the necessity of instant obedience. Unite firm-
> ness with gentleness. Let your children always
> understand that you mean what you say. Never
> promise them unless you are quite sure that you
> can give them what you say. If you tell a lit-
> tle child to do something, show him how to do
> it, and see that it is done. Always punish
> your children for willful disobedience, but
> never punish them in anger. Never let them
> perceive that they vex you or make you lose
> your command. If they give way to petulance or
> ill temper, wait until they are calm, and then
> gently reason with them on the impropriety of
> their conduct . . .[6]

In January, 1867, Funk began publishing a series of
printed Bible lessons in the *Herald of Truth*. These included four each month and covered 32 points of Christian
doctrine for the purpose of furnishing religious instruction for the young and all who wished to study the Bible.
It is well known also that the simple Mennonite elementary schools scattered along the frontier always included
the Bible in their studies program. These steps helped
to prepare the way for the coming of the Sunday school
program which Funk was determined to promote.

The Sunday School Movement

The history of the Sunday school movement among Mennonites in America has been told by J. C. Wenger in *The
Church Nurtures Faith* (1963), which is an enlargement
and updating of an earlier manuscript by Harold S. Bender. In this account Wenger identifies the first Sunday
school as having convened in Waterloo County, Ontario,
in 1840, with others following sporadically until their
full acceptance in 1863. Funk himself had attended a

(non-Mennonite) Sunday school in Pennsylvania as a boy
and said later, "This Sunday school proved to be one of
the greatest blessings of my life."

In commenting on the origin of the Sunday school
movement among Mennonites Wenger acknowledges a certain
spiritual lethargy in the church of mid-nineteenth century America, but adds that competition from the so-
called "union Sunday school" establishments in many communities was a major factor in moving Mennonites to
initiate their own. Thus Wenger writes:

> Indeed it is not improbable that one of the
> largest sources of loss to the Mennonite
> church before the church began to have its
> own Sunday school was the union Sunday
> schools established in Mennonite communities.
> Through this avenue many thousands of lives
> were diverted to other denominations from
> the Mennonite church which needed them so
> badly. In fact, the unmistakable evidence of
> this before the eyes of ministers and parents
> awakened them to the danger and was one of the
> greatest causes for the establishment of the
> Sunday school in the Mennonite church.[7]

Opposition to the movement was severe, even leading
to divisions in Ohio, Ontario, Pennsylvania, Virginia,
and particularly the Old Order division with Jacob
Wisler in Indiana in 1872.

The reasons for the opposition went far beyond a
fear of the new. They included genuine concern for the
spiritual welfare of the church and for the preservation
of a precious heritage. It should be noted that Mennonite congregations were not the only ones opposed to
the Sunday school. Mennonites, however, had an additional cause for concern in that the schools meant a shift
from German to English in religious discourse in which
language and faith had thus far been seen as one. But
the objections went beyond tradition and language as the

following letter published in the *Herald of Truth* in 1870 indicates:

> We object to it because we find no Scripture for lay members to speak publicly in our churches. We object to it because it is a violation of the gospel to allow women to teach in our churches. We object to it because persons not members of our church are allowed to teach publicly in our churches which is unscriptural. We object to it because such sabbath schools are in fashion amongst the highest, the proudest, and the dressiest classes of our country, and following them we follow after something in high repute by the world and friendship with the world is enmity with God. We object to it because it is represented as teaching our youth the sacred Scripture only while there is a mixture of other books used along with them, made up of select matter from the Word of God in part, and partly as tales by societies not opposed to war, bloodshed, or imposing cost and inconvenience by suing at law. We object to it because the spirit of pride and exaltedness is being cultivated by giving the most progressive scholars marks of honors. We object to it because it is something new that has crept into our church . . .[8]

Nevertheless, Sunday schools continued to flourish across the Mennonite family of congregations. In assessing their contribution to Mennonite faith and practice Wenger identifies the following: (a) the Sunday school helped to keep Mennonite young people in the church; (b) it increased Bible knowledge; (c) it elevated spiritual life; (d) it raised the level of moral life, especially through the teaching of temperance; (e) it provided activity and new life in the church; (f) it created lay leadership; and (g) it was largely

responsible for the growth of the missionary movement.[9]
In summary Wenger (and Bender) feel that the Sunday
school was a significant factor in bringing about the
1890-1910 Great Awakening in the Mennonite Church.

The Sunday school did not present the same kind of
obstacle to the Mennonite emigrants from Russia. This
was true, in part, because the schools had by that time
become an accepted part of the American religious land-
scape and gradually found their way into Russian Mennonite circles. Some Russian Mennonite groups have not
accepted the Sunday school to this day and consider it
an alien and threatening movement, but their numbers
are relatively few.

It may be that interest in the Sunday school has
crested among Mennonites in North America and is on the
decline, particularly among young people and adults.
The reasons for this may be both cultural and spiritual.
Whether the newly published *Foundation Series* will turn
the tide in a positive direction again remains to be
seen.

Concluding Comments

The factors which shaped Anabaptist and Mennonite
approaches to nurturing the faith were historical,
social, and economic but also theological. It may be
that doctrine and identity concerns dominated. The
following categories are either explicit or implicit in
the preceding pages or can, in any case, be amply docu-
mented further.

First, persecution was the great over-arching factor
in the first generation, with continuing suffering and
harassment later. This experience had a profound impact
physically on where they ultimately located to find shel-
ter. This fleeing and hiding syndrome in turn led to
withdrawal from society and the consequent growth of
ethnicity and a shriveling of the missionary impulse.
As a subculture and counter-culture they were forced in-

to self-sufficiency in all areas of life, including education. Persecution also led to a deep struggle of and for identity--an unwanted heretical minority. Being the quiet in the land in relation to socio-political issues is but one of the legacies of this total experience. There are other legacies. Even doing good to those in need may have a compensatory, wanting to be loved ingredient in it. Persecution and minority status undoubtedly shaped Mennonites to this day as much as sixteenth century Anabaptist theology. All educational efforts need to take this factor into account. Can the negative legacies of persecution be overcome in our nurturing today?

Second, a believers' church theology probably calls for a more deliberate nurture program than the sacramental-liturgical tradition. There is a) the rejection of total depravity and affirmation of free will; there is b) the model of the church in the Bible, restitution-primitivism which, individually, calls for first generation kinds of experience-commitment and, collectively, calls for membership expectations that are formidable; there is c) the tension between conversion and nurture as rites of passage; there is d) the commitment to radically Bible-centered doctrine but without being obscurantist; there is e) a commitment to truth and a venerable heritage, but also to be open to work with and learn from other traditions; there is f) a counter-culture stance commitment in areas like peace and life-style, but also a commitment to live and witness in the midst of society; there is g) a commitment to both prophetic and to priestly ministries, etc. This theology becomes the context in which a believers' church approach to education must take shape and be tested.

Third, there is yet another element to be considered in constructing a believers' church educational model-- all the societal, economic, theological, and political forces among which we live in late twentieth century. Violence, oppressive dictatorships of the left and the

150

right, poverty, apocalypticism, the electronic religious media are the context in which Mennonites live and work today. It is also in this context that the church seeks to be faithful. This context, as well as Anabaptist-Mennonite history and theology, is part of the testing with which any proposed educational model will need to cope.

FOOTNOTES

[1] "Letters to Thomas Müntzer by Conrad Grebel and Friends," in *Spiritual and Anabaptist Writers.* Edited by George H. Williams and Angel M. Mergal. Vol. XXV, *The Library of Christian Classics.*, p. 80.

[2] Henry C. Vedder, *Balthasar Hubmaier.* New York: G. P. Putnam's Sons, 1905., p. 77.

[3] In John H. Yoder's, *The Legacy of Michael Sattler.* Scottdale: Herald Press, 1973., pp. 150-177.

[4] In William R. Estep, Jr., *Anabaptist Beginnings (1523-1533).* Nieuwkopp: B. De Graaf, 1976, p. 82.

[5] Heinhold Fast, "Hans Krüsis Büchlein über Glauben und Taufe" in Cornelius J. Dyck, editor, *A Legacy of Faith.* Newton, Kansas: Faith and Life Press, 1962, pp. 213-231.

[6] Quoted in J. E. Hartzler, *Education Among the Mennonites of America.* Danvers, Illinois: Central Mennonite Publishing Board, 1925., p. 72.

[7] J. C. Wenger, *The Church Nurtures Faith.* Scottdale, Pa: Herald Press, 1963., p. 27.

[8] *Ibid.*, p. 38.

[9] For an empirical test of the validity of these claims among members of five Mennonite/Brethren in Christ denominations, see J. Howard Kauffman and Leland Harder, *Anabaptists Four Centuries Later.* Scottdale: Herald Press, 1975., Chapter 12, "Christian Education in the Local Church," pp. 199-218.

RESPONSES TO THE PAPER

Leland Harder: I've heard many words of appreciation for the papers being presented at this seminar and for the formal responses by persons who barely received them and had to collect their thoughts enroute. And now for the responses to C. J.'s paper, we'll call on the persons sitting at the table in order of their chairs: Don, Linea, Anne, and Arnoldo.

Don Augsburger: I have always admired C. J.'s keen insight and understanding. My response will seek to take seriously Leland's guidelines to reflect on the input of the presenters in the light of our own experience and congregational perspectives. Last Thursday as I went to a teaching assignment in Lancaster, I stopped at the Mellinger Church, where I became a member of the Lancaster Conference many years ago, as a renegade from Ohio. I remember how they presented my name and a brother jumped up and said, "But how does he really feel about the discipline, and is his wife in the order of the church?" It got very quiet and a dear bishop brother jumped up and said, "We've talked to him and he's more in favor of a lot of these things than some of you." In that church, of course, we had to deal with things like the frock coat and the radio. In spite of the pain of change, I came out with a deep appreciation for the Mennonite heritage; but I have to keep asking myself, "What does this say to people who do not have this heritage?" We now have 670,000 worldwide membership, half of whom do not have this heritage. How do we nurture the faith in relation to some of the themes of this seminar like historical continuity and identity? I happen to have that continuity and identity, my name is in the Mennonite Encyclopedia, and I come from Switzerland, where I understand they once found a baby on a doorstep and called him an Augsburger. We went back there, and all we found was an Augsburger Publishing business; but when I asked whether there were any Augsburgers around, they laughed at me. My wife's name was Kling, and the phone book was full of Klings. In the Mellinger Church, too, things are changing. J. C. Wenger spoke on "Human and Divine Dimensions of the Scriptures," and when I came out of the Conference meeting and turned on the religious radio station WDAC with its fundamentalist approach, I saw in a moment what one of the ministers said to me, "How can we deal with what's happening to our people by these constant influences from both ends of the continuum?" Like we just heard C. J. saying, if it's isolation, we lose our vision; if it's assimilation, we lose our witness.

In my home church in Elida, Ohio, they knew the name Menno Simons and assimilated by osmosis some of the things that came down from past generations; but I suppose they did more in-fighting than many and yet produced thirty to forty bishops and ministers and deacons. The previous generation, except for my older brother, has pretty much left that church. But the next generation for some reason or another seemed to hang in there, they had a change in leadership, and there emerged a congregation of people who really seem to care about each other. That church used to be the center of community life. In his analysis, Grant Stoltzfus said then the center became the courthouse and finally the shopping center. We had a deacon brother by the name of Solly Brunk, who was really the bishop; and he lived through all of those schisms. It was a sort of "peace shall destroy many" kind of church. We lived right next to Solly, and the question in our home was often not "What would God think?" but "What would Solly think?" At least I grew up sensing that there was more than one way to do a thing right and wanting somehow to prove to Solly that there was more than one way to do a thing right. We got a radio and played it in the car on the south side of the house so that Solly wouldn't hear it. In spite of that kind of mentality, I grew up with a deep appreciation of the church. I think it was Sim Huber who asked me to teach the Sunday school class. Sim would stand you up there before the class, and then you would teach it; and I remember how my knees shook. He was a person who cared, and those are the kinds of things I remember; and even though they didn't know much about the Anabaptist story, they nurtured our faith. My great grandfather, J. M. Shenk, had been bishop there before he died when I was about ten years old. And when Solly died and I returned for the funeral, I went out to the graveyard and stood at J. M.'s grave with tears in my eyes and said, "Solly's gone. I hope you're together." They fought like dogs and cats, but they were trying to hold on to something and transmit something of great importance to them. They were isolated and had lost some of the right kind of vision. They feared assimilation like the plague and stayed away from it. When I'm back there, I'm considered liberal; but when I came to Indiana, I was usually considered more conservative. As one moves across the church, one has to try to fit in where you are. It keeps me wrestling with the two major themes of this paper: our continuity and our identity.

Linea Geiser: Needless to say, my experience is very different; and I'm going to speak out of my experience also. I resonated very much with this paper and could spend hours talking about all it has triggered in me. One of my first "hurrahs" was for a positive word on humanism. I don't know what happens when I go into a congregation to talk about child development and faith development, and they say, "That sounds like secular humanism." I thought it sounded like Christianity. Now to find out that humanism is a part of our past and that it led to biblical renewal and moral reform sounds good to me and has given me a bit of new ammunition.

Coming from a Dutch Mennonite tradition and from Russian Mennonite sources, I found it hard when I came to Goshen College to understand the different way of looking at everything. As I read this paper, and its discussion of differences in emphasis on subjects like conversion, I can better understand my past as well as the past of other Goshen College students.

Also as I read I wondered, "Can the New Testament Church be restored?", which was something the early Anabaptists were working on. I understood very little of last night's presentation, but I think I know enough to know that you can never go back, that when you re-vision and re-member, it's always different from the past. And so I wonder about re-visioning and re-membering first century Christianity, what that can mean.

Another response is the feeling that many lay people in Mennonite congregations really do believe in original sin and really do want their children converted at the earliest age and baptized as soon as possible. How do we get the courage to trust God who gave us freedom of will, and trust our children that it doesn't all have to happen by the age of twelve. When C. J. said that the Bibles of our forebears included the Apocrypha, I pondered why I had to reach the age of 45 before I ever read any part of the Apocrypha, and why it has not been part of our literature of instruction. I am reading it this semester here at Seminary, and it has helped me to understand the canon much better and has given me a more realistic attitude toward the Scripture.

Another small aside concerns the importance of music in transmitting the faith, and the importance of the Ausbund as a teaching tool. I'm concerned about the kind of theology conveyed in our music, in the hymns we sing.

Another neat thing about this paper was the historical flow of who was in charge of the religious instruction of youth--now the home; then the schools take over and the church doesn't have to do anything; then the schools aren't there and the responsibility returns to the home, especially in a pioneering situation; then it settles down to comfortable living and nurture is turned over again to the schools or the college or the seminary. I wondered what persecution today would do to this flow.

Finally, just a few reflections on the Sunday school movement. I used to think it was one of the most wonderful things that happened in the Mennonite Church. Now I'm with C.J.; I'm not so sure. I'm concerned that we may be freezing our theology at a child's level. Do we have year-after-year learning, or one year repeated over and over? As a curriculum writer, how do I write materials that will not close off further learning? By way of relating all four papers so far, perhaps storytelling is one way, to tell the stories of faith, without hanging morals on them, so that the story can teach and teach and teach.

Anne Rupp: Not to repeat what others have said, I'd like to focus on just two areas of concern. The first is the struggle with diversity that seems to characterize Anabaptist and Mennonite history, as people tried to discover the essence and meaning of the New Testament faith. The admonition that comes out of this is that we shouldn't too easily conclude what needs to be concluded. This applies to the struggle with diversity even within out traditional churches but even more so among our younger churches where people are coming from many different backgrounds and each person has a different understanding of what the Christian faith is all about. When we talk about being a "counter-culture" in that kind of a situation, we're faced with a real challenge because the tradition-al church may find it hard to be a counter-culture that is really alive, and the younger churches with their diversity may find it very hard to get together on who in the congregation is going to be in charge.

In connection with my assignment to write a leader's guide for the last of the Foundation Series, I heard Dale Brown of Bethany Seminary speak on being led by Word and Spirit, which gave me another whole perspective on the meaning of Anabaptist faith and life for today. When C. J. refers to the "loss of vision" and again on "the dangers of legalism," it made me aware again that the struggle of the book of Galatians is always with us and that we need to continue to find out what it means to be led by the Word and by the Spirit. It is always easier to interpret the New Testament as a form of legalism than to be open to the Spirit of God, because we can't legislate the Spirit.

Arnoldo Casas: I perceive that history has played a very important part in the Mennonite Church and the development of the Mennonite community. And as often as I participate in workshops like this, it seems that we always jump from one point of history to another, like from 1525 to 1982. As a contrast to that, I was delighted to hear Peter last night with such a different interpretation of history, dealing with another period of time, using Latin terminology that relates to the background from which I come, the Latin background of the Roman Catholic Church. The history that C. J. is talking about has become more familiar to me and I can identify with some of it, but I do not hear enough about the other parts of my history that relate to other backgrounds.

When I visited some of the German-speaking Mennonite colonies in Latin Ameri-ca, I became aware of how past persecutions have led to their isolation from the world, and why perhaps when I became a Mennonite that was one of the first things I was taught. But then I began to ask how this theology of separation I was taught relates to another part of our theology, to share the Gospel, to be a witness in the world, to be a disciple of Christ, to be a person who goes and preaches about peace and who serves the needs of his neighbors. Perhaps Mennon-ites have such a hard problem relating to minorities because they have been a minority in the world. I don't really like the word, minority, because it seems minorities are always majorities within their own group in order to survive. That leads to a false basis of identity. At the airport in Bolivia, one of the pilots took a little package on board and told the co-pilot, "I have a present for you." "What is it?" he asked. "Why don't you open it?" he said. So he opened it, and it was cheese. Then the pilot said, "This is the best cheese you will find in Bolivia. It is Mennonite cheese. And it will be better when we get to Miami if you eat it with a good German meal."

Last night, C. J. was commenting that we need to edit a lot of history, and to do so in relation to the reality of Jesus Christ and his relation to human cultures of all groups.

Leland Harder: Thank you very much, Don, Linea, Anne, and Arnoldo. Well, we were supposed to have our small group reports eight minutes ago. I'm not a very good timekeeper. We'll have our small groups yet this morning, but we won't have time for their report-backs. We're going to do small group work tonight in lieu of the report by the task force, which never got written. I'm going to suggest now before we disperse that C. J. take another minute or two to respond to these responses.

C. J. Dyck: I appreciate the responses and without trying to be a cop-out I'll make just a few comments. Arnoldo is exactly right that we need to edit our history. We need increasingly to develop a global consciousness and theology. It was out of this consciousness that the 1981 revision of Introduction to Mennonite History was produced. One of my goals for that revision was to take all the sexist language out. Another was to do justice to the so-called minority groups that have become a part of our history. So I think you are exactly right.

I also think we should be aware that Mennonites have always taken the Bible very seriously, and that consequently their history has almost become their theology. There is nothing wrong with being ethnic insofar as all people are ethnic. Our basic question, rather, is how, given our ethnicity, each new generation can be a new act of God. We ought not to be so naive as to act as if we had no history or ethnicity. Perhaps Wilhelm Dilthey, who lived in the 19th century, can help us when he talked about a "lived history" in which it becomes a way of life incorporated within us without becoming a yardstick that measures everything, and which is open to all kinds of new influences that shape us. Like Sojourners magazine, which sounds very much like a believers' church kind of theology. And like some of our urban churches, that are forming inclusive kinds of believers' congregations. The variety of grace is like the variety of nature. If God can create thousands of different kinds of flowers, there can be thousands of different ways people come to God and are nurtured in the faith.

Leland Harder: As we return to our small groups, let's see if we can begin to envision a model of Christian education that can integrate the variety of grace we have experienced so far in this workshop.

A HISPANIC PERSPECTIVE

Rafael Falcón

To speak in representation of an ethnic group, composed of hundreds of thousands of persons--20 million
in the United States alone--is rather presumptuous and
daring. Yet I will attempt to offer as nearly accurately as possible an interpretation of the nurture of
faith from a Hispanic perspective. To accomplish this
goal, I will utilize personal experiences, which undoubtedly remain the most credible and concrete evidence in any debate, reinforced further by a panoramic
exploration of the ethnic group to which I belong.

Aibonito, Puerto Rico, the mecca of Puerto Rican
Mennonitism, was the place of my birth several years ago.
The Mennonites had begun their work in La Plata, a rural
community close to Aibonito, during World War II, but
it was not until 1955 that I came into contact with them
when some neighbors of ours invited my parents to attend
their church. My parents accepted their invitation and
their decision to continue became a determining factor
in my life, since from that time on, my spiritual involvement has been with the Mennonite Church.

Shortly after their conversion, my parents decided
to send me to a Mennonite school in nearby Pulguillas
named Academia Menonita Betania. When I started attending the school, as a third grader, I realized that
there was a great difference between this school and
the Catholic academy I had been attending up to that
point. My first Christian teacher was Patricia Brenne-
man Santiago, a VSer, who gave many positive examples

for my spiritual life and intellect. Other exemplary
teachers and Bible classes at the school further
deepened my spiritual knowledge as a child. Participation in small groups and choruses gave me the experience in expression of my growing faith. I remember
with warm memories the chapel periods where all the
elementary grades would gather in worship.

Inclusive in this impressionable stage of my life
should be mentioned the influence of my friends and
their families. The Hispanic culture with a keen
awareness of that influence of friendship upon the
individual has cleverly coined the adage: "Tell me
with whom you associate and I will tell you who you
are."

When I was thirteen years old my family and I
attended an evangelistic campaign, and it was here where
I made a public confession of faith. At fifteen years
of age, I was baptized. I would like to emphasize that
this concrete and public decision was not a sudden unexpected event, but rather a climax to a series of
reverberating occurrences beginning with the early
Betania experiences, a time of nurture and development
of my Christian faith.

Unfortunately, since Betania offered classes only
through the ninth grade, it was necessary for me to
move into the public school system for my high school
experience. Needless to say, after having been in an
academic environment characterized by its Christian
beliefs, it was a drastic change for me. I had to
learn how to relate with my new classmates without
entering into their life of drinking, dancing, gam-
bling and dirty conversation. These three years of
high school served as a test for which I had practiced
for seven years in my Mennonite alma mater. The spiritual foundation laid during those years served to
bring me through the more difficult times. I will
always remember, however, the stamp that was placed on
one for being Mennonite or Protestant, a label that

would sometimes isolate the "offender." For me, this became the preface for other experiences that were to come later on in my work and further studies, times when I would be put under constant fire for what I believed. These encounters in the nonchristian world are significant since they can become either constructive or destructive, leading one toward a challenge and new understanding or toward a marring of Christian values. These experiences are to the Christian much like a doctoral dissertation is to a graduate student: that which separates the men from the boys.

While in high school I sensed within me the development of the ability to direct and organize groups. I began to accept positions as assistant to the Sunday school teacher of the junior-high class, as a teacher in vacation Bible school, as president of the youth group and other responsibilities. These opportunities further strengthened my faith, giving me the confidence that I could serve within the church structure, and as a result, I grew spiritually.

After graduation from high school, I decided to attend a college of Presbyterian origin, approximately 70 miles away from home. In the three years that it took me to acquire my B.A., I discovered that this school, not unlike many others, had lost the Christian foundation for which it had been established. I also realized that I had to work just as hard in this place to keep my faith nurtured, as if I had gone to a state university.

After graduation, even though I received offers from other schools, I decided to go back to Betania, my alma mater, to work. It was a pleasure to return to my roots, to the place of spiritual nurture for me as a child, and to work with people who shared the same values as mine. Nevertheless it was also a challenge because I went back not as a student, but as a member of the faculty, an example to students and a pillar of the institution. It was now my responsibility to do

with my students what others had done for me. But I
was not alone: every morning before the students
arrived, faculty and staff would meet for a devotional
and prayer. And from these scheduled daily half-hour
sessions came support, encouragement, challenges and
inspiration--fertile ground for nurture and growth.

After two years at Betania, an offer of a position
available in a very poor section of Aibonito lured me
into acceptance of a teaching job there. My friends
made no bones of it but told me point-blank that I was
crazy since the school had a bad reputation for disci-
plinary problems among the students--even pulled knives.
In reflection upon this stage of my life I remember with
real warmth (and some humor) the fact that the faculty
and personnel realized that I was "different"--I could
pray. After this ability was recognized, I was used
regularly for invocations and benedictions in the significant occasions of the school such as graduation,
parent-teacher meetings, faculty meetings, etc.

Later, thanks to God's leading and through a selec-
tive scholarship, I was given one government-paid year
of graduate studies in the University of Puerto Rico.
Since the university was very large, the range of
ideologies among the students was very broad. One
could find advocates of socialism and island independence. There were the charismatics, the atheists, the
none-involved. And there were also the earnest students, involved in their own world. This year of my
life was more a time of sharing, a plateau of evalua-
tion.

During the second half of this year I married an
alumnus of Goshen College, Christine Yoder, who has
helped me greatly in strengthening my life spiritually,
as well as intellectually. After finishing the year of
graduate studies, I moved again into the world of
Christian education by accepting an administrative position in the school in which I had studied and taught,
the Academia Menonita Betania.

While directing the school there for three years, I kept thinking about continuing graduate studies to prepare myself more academically. I decided on the University of Iowa, where I was offered a teaching assistantship along with my studies. It was a significant decision to leave my tropically refreshing Enchanted Island for 28 years to move to the new world of the Corn State where hot is hot and cold is cold. There in the University of Iowa, I was required again to put into practice that which I had already experienced in high school, during my under-graduate and graduate studies, and in my public school teaching-- faith in action with both feet on the ground. Once again, the faith nurtured years ago in my childhood school experience energized the strength within me to defend and act upon my spiritual beliefs and values.

We lived in Iowa for a period of three years, during which time I completed all the courses necessary for a doctoral degree. We attended the First Mennonite Church of Iowa City, which at that time was pastored by Ed Stoltzfus. Three elements stand out in my mind concerning our church experience. First was the excellent children's Sunday school department in which our eldest son was then involved. Second were the individuals who provided friendship and support in spite of my rigid student schedule. And third was the availability of our pastor, his concern for us and his unfaltering support of my personal value to the church-at-large, even if time did not permit me to give fully to the local congregation.

In July 1979 we moved to Goshen where I now work jointly teaching in the Foreign Language Department and directing the Hispanic Ministries Department at Goshen College.

God has been good to me. He has opened avenues, permitting me to prepare myself and serve in an area of life which I consider very important--that of Christian education, an academic yet spiritual education. There

is no doubt within me that my desire is to serve God
with the gift he has given me, that of teaching and
working with young people. In this area of work, I am
able to aid in the nurture of others' faith in a similar
way to which others have done for me.

Through my spiritual pilgrimage, which is very
likely not similar to many Continental Hispanics, or
Latin Americans, can be perceived certain elements that
have been instrumental in the nurture of my faith:
(1) early education in a Christian institution, (2)
teachers with techniques and convictions, (3) friends
and companions with similar Christian values, (4) opportunities for spiritual fortification in environments
not analogous to my principles, (5) occasions to serve
in the Church, and finally but not ultimately, (6) my
family, wife and my parents. It should be emphasized
that this process of nurture has been slow and oppor-
tune, somewhat similar to the aging that goes into the
making of good wine.

I believe the last element mentioned should be examined in greater depth. It is unquestionable that my
parents have played an important role in the nurture of
my faith. To see my parents interested in the Christian faith, in the life of the church, and to see their
faithfulness and participation in the services and
church activities has been an inspiration to my faith.
Even today I will receive letters of spiritual encouragement from my mother, animating and supporting me.
Without a doubt, the parent-child relationship and the
home influence upon the child should be a point of
significant concentration in this study of the nurture
of faith, no matter the ethnic orientation.

And now I am going to take the risk--as the second
and the most enterprising part of my presentation--to
try to unravel this phenomenon from a generic Hispanic
point of view. This becomes a daring venture since I
am only one Puerto Rican who has come to the States a
mere six years ago, making it very possible that a

Mexican-American (Chicano) or Puerto Rican-American
(Neo-Rican) may have a totally different vision from my
own. This task becomes increasingly more difficult
since the nurture of faith is not being considered in
this study from the angle of a more ethnically solid
cultural group such as in Argentina or Ecuador, but
from the very amalgamous angle of the Hispanics within
the United States, who share one language but have certain cultural differences.

The Hispanic Mennonite Church in the United States
is the one group within our denomination credited with
the greatest numeric growth during the last few years.
This is understandably so because it is a church
directed toward evangelism, clearly following the mandate, "Go ye into all the world and preach the gospel,"
but it is also a church lacking a standard of how to
nurture the faith of those evangelized. It is possible
that our leaders, lacking the technique or the academic
background to cope with this new challenge, will present to the Hispanic Church a similar situation as the
historical example which occurred during the Mexican
Revolution. In this political case, the Mexican people
successfully overthrew the famous dictator Porfirio
Diaz . . . for what? They opened the situation for
anarchy, the sad predicament of a people who were not
equipped to work with what they had obtained.

The Anglo Mennonite can speak of his grandfather
who was a bishop in Pennsylvania in 1880, but the
majority of the Hispanic Mennonites cannot move much
farther than the historical moment of their own personal spiritual pilgrimage. There is little drawing
upon the resources of past experience, literature or
church life to nurture the faith of the young Hispanic
church community. It is my opinion that the majority
of our people are limited to a spiritual milk diet, not
by virtue of desire but availability. Comes into focus
then, the increasingly potent question: what happens
to the Hispanic Christian who wants to nurture his
faith with spiritual meat? This presents the very sen-

sitive dichotomy of the recent covert vs. the more
mature member where the former outranks the latter.
Branching from this challenge comes a possible dis-
quieting issue: is it possible to evangelize and nurture the faith at the same time, without sacrificing
one or the other?

Besides the aforementioned challenges to the spiritual growth and nurture of the Hispanic Christian in the
United States can be added the social pressures of
racial discrimination, language problems, inadequacy in
housing and jobs, and others. Our Hispanic Mennonite
population, which is currently in great transition,
must however, grapple with more basic issues--family
relationships and qualified instruction nurturing Christian roots. I would like to strongly emphasize that a
positive growth in these basic elements would not im-
munize the Hispanic believer against attacks on the
nurture of his faith, but would, without a shadow of a
doubt, place another stone in the building of our
spiritual house. The effect of a strong model of faith
in the home and a solid Christian education attractively
planned by the home congregation and church institutions
will accompany the believer through the rest of his life
and will remain alive, although sometimes subconsciously,
to aid in the varied situations of life--at least, such
has been my experience.

PERSPECTIVES ON THE CHRISTIAN NURTURE
OF THE POWERLESS-OPPRESSED[1]

John A. Rogers

Methodological

1. "The mission of Christ creates its own church.
Mission does not come from the church; it is from mission and in the light of mission that the church has to
be understood."[2]

2. The end of Christian nurture is to precipitate/
facilitate participation in the mission of Christ.

3. Method in Christian education reflects world
view. Therefore, inadequacy of method may suggest an
inadequacy of world view. However, it is possible to
change method without changing world view. This suggests
that the critique of method should include identifying
the underlying world view and evaluating it relative to
the mission of Christ, one's perception of which is an
aspect of one's world view. Failure to identify and
critique the underlying world view of a system of nurture may result in replacing one inadequate method with
another fundamentally inadequate method--though the
latter may be an advance on the former.

4. The mission of Christ includes the liberation of
the oppressed, the empowerment of the powerless.[3]
Liberation-empowerment is God's method of moving the
creation toward self-fulfillment, that is, the ultimate
realization of God's intention for the creation.[4]

5. Liberation-empowerment is a means of transcendence for both the oppressed and their oppressors--
the socially, politically, and economically powerful.
It moves both toward true self-actualization. (See
item twelve below.)

6. Any method of Christian nurture must take
seriously the divine agenda of liberation-empowerment.
Failure to do so precludes Christocentric self-
actualization, which is an (intermediate) aim of
Christian nurture. This precipitates/facilitates a
closedness of world view, which prevents God's precipi-
tating our becoming (development) through historical
events, which are the means for the realization of God's
agenda.

(One might legitimately question whether the above
assumptions deal primarily with method or with content.
The following two assumptions suggest that they are
essentially methodological.)

7. Christian nurture is fundamentally experiential.
If the end of nurture is participation in the mission
of Christ, which results in self-actualization, then
commitment is an intermediate end--or, perhaps, the
ultimate means--of Christian nurture. Commitment is
engendered by experiencing the viability of Christian
existence through others. The cognitive element of
Christian nurture, then, explains/interprets the experiential.

Certainly the distinction between "experiential" and
"cognitive" is semantic, for the nature of experience is
determined by interpretation; the cognitive is an inherent element of the experiential.

The knowing subject and the object to be known
[experience to be shared] must be seen in their
historical context, . . . objective knowledge
is always dependent . . . on the standpoint
of the subject. This means that any cognitive

act establishes its object. Any object is
only an object when it is the object of a
subject. Cognition always stresses a particular aspect of reality and leaves many other
aspects obscure. It includes and excludes,
limits and delimits. Even objective knowledge is historically conditioned, provisional,
and in principle never complete.[5]

On the other hand, the cognitive is relatively in-
comprehensible apart from the experiential. That is,
persons need practical paradigms for understanding what
is taught. The meaning of what is imparted verbally is
determined by the examples that are provided; and apart
from concrete examples, what is imparted is subject to
a multitude of misinterpretations. Note, for example,
Jesus' instructions to his followers: "I give you a
new commandment: love one another; as I have loved you,
so you are to love one another;" "This is my commandment: love one another, as I have loved you. There is
no greater love than this, that a man should lay down
his life for his friends" (John 13:34; 15:12-13, NEB).

8. Christian nurture is fundamentally dialogical.
We recognize the incompleteness of our experiences and
knowledge. Thus the aim of Christian nurture is not
the replication per se of particular experiences and
knowledge but commitment that leads to self-
actualization through participation in the mission of
Christ. We also recognize that the mission of Christ
is in process and that it is being furthered both quan-
titatively and qualitatively, that is, that the mission
of Christ is furthered by the numerical growth of the
church and by the gifts/abilities that persons bring
to the church. Thus we are open to God's utilizing a
generation or a group to reorient the church so that it
is more truly aligned with the mission of Christ. This
demands an openness to dialoguing around new experiences
that individuals, groups, or the entire community faces.

Thomas Ogletree reflects an underlying assumption for this dialogical emphasis:

> The theologian [or the church in general] cannot choose his own agenda--certainly not on the basis of personal preferences, but also not simply in terms of problems residing in the theological tradition as such. Christian theology continually receives its agenda from the world, from the pressures, the thrusts, and the collisions of worldly developments, for it is only in relation to these developments that it can express and serve the Christian promise to men. The relevant developments are by no means always or even characteristically focused in the life and activity of the self-conscious community of faith . . . no actually existing human community can contain or even adequately serve the creative, transforming energy which the reality of Jesus Christ has released and continues to release in the midst of human history . . . [Thus,] the final test of the church's faithfulness is not that it always be in the forefront of every creative new thrust in human history, but that it ever learn anew to read the "signs of the times," to discern "what God is doing in the world and to join his work."[6]

Liberation-Empowerment

9. Liberation-empowerment is fundamentally a matter of world view. Though we cannot disregard the effects of coercion--whether social, political, or economic-- the determination of world view is the most efficient means of manipulation.

10. The powerless-oppressed are most susceptible to this type of manipulation--except what is provided by those who exercise power within the system.

One of the most debilitating results of moderni-
zation is a feeling of powerlessness in the face
of institutions controlled by those whom we do
not know and whose values we often do not
share . . . Upper-income people already have
ways to resist the encroachment of megastruc-
tures. It is not their children who are at the
mercy of alleged child experts, not their health
which is endangered by miscellaneous vested
interests, not their neighborhoods which are
made playthings of utopian planners. Upper-
income people may allow themselves to be
victimized on all these scores, but they have
ways to resist if they choose to resist. Poor
people have this power to a much lesser degree.[7]

And since the means for definition and preservation
are not indigenous--and thereby not reflecting the interests of the powerless-oppressed--and since Western
capitalist values and priorities are generally con-
trary to the liberating, empowering, and self-actualizing
paradigm provided by Jesus, we may assume that the means
provided/prescribed by the socially, politically, and
economically powerful are nonfacilitative of genuine
liberation-empowerment.

The ordinary person is crushed, diminished, converted into a spectator, maneuvered by myths
which powerful social forces have created.
These myths turn against him; they destroy and
annihilate him . . . Gradually, without even
realizing the loss, he relinquishes his
capacity for choice; he is expelled from the
orbit of decisions. Ordinary men do not
perceive the tasks of the time; the latter
are interpreted by an "elite" and presented
in the form of recipes, of prescriptions.
And when men try to save themselves by following prescriptions, they drown in leveling
anonymity, without hope and without faith,
domesticated and adjusted.[8]

The point is that since those who determine values
and impose them on the powerless-oppressed are concerned
with maintaining the system that works to their advantage, those liberating-empowering devices that they propose will reflect their ultimate intent to preserve the
system. Thus the essence of their proposals for
liberation-empowerment will be the subordination of the
powerless-oppressed to the existing system, which preci-
pitates powerlessness.

11. The radicalness of Jesus lay, in part, in the
new paradigm for liberation-empowerment that he provided, wherein he subverted the paradigms of the powers
that be. Recognizing the inherent weaknesses of existing paradigms of liberation-empowerment, he provided a
new paradigm not essentially circumscribed by a concern
for systemic maintenance. He thereby indicated that
liberation-empowerment (self-actualization) lay in
transcending existing systemically oriented paradigms
(interpret Luke 4:18-19 in light of this perspective).

The issue relative to Christian nurture is, can the
church get beyond its interest in self-preservation and
systemic maintenance to participation in the divine
agenda of liberation-empowerment? A genuine liberation-
empowerment agenda cannot be imposed by those who do not
share the life-space of the powerless-oppressed. Thus
if the church is to share in the liberation agenda of
Christ, it must identify with the powerless-oppressed
in their struggle for liberation-empowerment.

12. This identification with the powerless-oppressed
is essential for the ultimate self-actualization of the
church. Apart from this, there is no getting beyond un-
critical self-affirmation, which is not to be confused
with self-actualization. There is only existence as
ecclesia incurvata in se.

One takes for granted the basic structure [of
the ecclesiastical system] and moves on to
develop its size, power, and efficacy to the

utmost limits. If something does not function
well, it is because the system has not increased its power to the proper level at that
point . . . We ignore the fact that if the
basic system is irrational [or not liberating-
empowering] and structurally faulty, greater
power only accentuates its condition . . .
the increase of power in a sick system can
only produce unexpected forms of its own de-
rangement and eventually its downfall.[9]

Apart from an identification with the powerless-
oppressed, the church cannot fulfill its vocation. We
move toward comprehending the meaning of our existence
in Christ only as we participate in Christ's agenda,
even though this may demand risking a cherished self-
identity (see Matthew 16:24-25, NEB). Failure to accept the risk of participation results in alienation
relative to God, ourselves, our fellow humanity, and
the material world.[10]

13. Possible objectives for Black Christian nurture
include the following:

a. To study the dialogue in Black theology, in
the context of the Christian faith, in order to help
persons become aware of God as revealed in Jesus Christ,
the Liberator.

b. To understand other religious faiths of Black
people--Islam (faith of Muslims), African traditional
religions, humanism and secularism.

c. To help Black people know who they are and what
their human situation is in the American society.

d. To enable persons to investigate and evaluate
the historical Black religious experience, beginning
with Africa, through slavery, into the contemporary
urban society, and to seek its relevance for life today.

e. To help Blacks fulfill their liberating role as disciples of Christ in the world.

f. To share with White Americans, and all God's people, the God-given Black perspective of the Christian faith.

g. To enable and equip Black children, Black youth and Black adults to discover their divinely created human potential.

h. To utilize religious education as a major tool for liberation, freedom and justice in the American society.

i. To design a broad based educational program that aims at helping Blacks remedy the past deficiencies in American society and the Church and become a dynamic part of the process that directs the forces of change toward just and human ends.

j. To stimulate Blacks to engage in sharing, from the Black experience and perspective, meanings, values and purposes and power, with ourselves and others in a world where constructive sharing is the only alternative to mutual destruction.

k. To equip Blacks with those skills and strategies that influence those responsible for today's critical decisions and choices, thereby controlling the present and creating the future that Black Americans want.[11]

FOOTNOTES

[1]The essay of which these theses are a precis was written in the summer of 1981 as an attempt to articulate my perspectives on the task of the Christian nurture of the powerless-oppressed in America. The task force giving leadership to this seminar-workshop has the complete copy of the essay.

[2]Jürgen Moltmann, *The Church in the Power of the Spirit: A Contribution to Messianic Ecclesiology*, trans. by Margaret Kohl (New York: Harper & Row, 1977), p. 10.

[3]For a treatment of "empowerment" that is consistent with Anabaptist theology, see Thomas Ogletree, "Power and Human Fulfillment," *Pastoral Psychology* 22 (September 1971) 42-53; idem. "The Gospel as Power: Explorations in a Theology of Social Change," in *New Theology No. 8*, ed. by Martin E. Marty and Dean G. Peerman (New York: Macmillan Co., 1971), pp. 173-209.

[4]See Herbert O. Edwards, "The Third World and the Problem of God-Talk," *Harvard Theological Review* 64 (October 1971) 525-539; Helmut Gollwitzer, "Liberation in History," *Interpretation* 28 (October 1974) 404-421.

[5]Hans Küng, *Does God Exist? An Answer for Today*, trans. by Edward Quinn (Garden City, NY: Doubleday & Co., 1980), pp. 29-30.

[6]Ogletree, "The Gospel as Power," pp. 177-178.

[7]Peter L. Berger and Richard John Neuhaus, *To Empower People: The Role of Mediating Structures in Public Policy* (Washington: American Enterprise Institute for Public Policy Research, 1977), pp. 7-8; see

Edward Barnes, "The Black Community as the Source of Positive Self-Concept for Black Children: A Theoretical Perspective," in *Black Psychology*, ed. by Reginald Jones (New York: Harper & Row, 1972), pp. 166-192.

[8]Paulo Freire, *Education for Critical Consciousness* (New York: Seabury Press, Continuum Books, 1973), p. 6.

[9]Rubem Alves, *Tomorrow's Child: Imagination, Creativity, and the Rebirth of Culture* (New York: Harper & Row, 1972), pp. 4-5.

[10]Jurgen Moltmann, "The Hope of Resurrection and the Practice of Liberation," in idem, *The Future of Creation: Collected Essays*, trans. by Margaret Kohl (Philadelphia: Fortress Press, 1979), pp. 97-114.

[11]Olivia Pearl Stokes, "Education in the Black Church: Design for Change," *Religious Education* 69 (July-August 1974) 437-438.

RESPONSES TO THE PAPERS

Levi Miller: *These papers are quite different in their approaches. The one was quite personal, the other more conceptual. The one was more concrete, the other more theoretical. I'm going to respond to them in that same kind of way.*

I read Rafael's paper in Aibonito, Puerto Rico, of all places! I read it one night after accompanying a group of Mennonites who were singing in the Mennonite hospital in Aibonito. There was one woman in that crowd of singers who had Falcon written on her hymnbook, and she looked like Rafael. Later I discovered that it was Anna Melandez, Rafael's mother. Later, at the Puerto Rico convention which I was attending, there was a rehearsal of the story of the Puerto Rican Mennonite Church, and they were asking the questions, "Who are we?" "Where are we going?" And "What is our mission?" Various people got up and talked of the difficult times during the 40s and 50s, and then Anna Melandez said, "In 1955 I received God in this building. He called me to serve him, and that is our mission. I keep on serving him because he is wonderful with me, and it is beautiful to see brothers and sisters united." I talked with her afterward and mentioned that I had read her son's paper. Seeing her and talking with her, I was struck with the fact that Rafael could not have been otherwise.

Having said that, however (and I think it fits in well with what you said about the importance of the family as well as the church in the nurturing of faith), I was struck also with the similarities of his experiences with my own. Stripped of some of the language and cultural differences, Rafael's story could be my own-- the story he told of the Bible school and the Sunday school and the elementary school, the home influence, the worship experience, the modeling of the teacher, the evangelistic services, all remind me of contexts in my own life.

He ends up, however, mentioning various problems which Hispanic Christians are confronting--social pressures, racial discrimination, language barriers, inadequacy of housing and jobs, etc. It would be interesting to hear Rafael reflect on John's paper as a conceptual strategy for approaching issues like these.

I was impressed, John, by the thoughtfulness that went into your theses, the short form of the longer essay written earlier, and by your attempt to place liberation and empowerment at the center of the church's mission and seeing the nurturing of faith in the context of mission. I'm challenged because in so many ways I am unable to identify with the powerless and oppressed, and I think collectively most Mennonites sitting around these tables have this same problem. On one hand, these things are deeply engrained in the Amish-Mennonite psyche. I remember some of the songs from the Ausbund that we used to sing, and over half of them celebrated the martyrs. On the surface we should be able to identify with oppressed people, but I don't think we can because basically we have become a people of privilege. For six generations my own family lived on the land in Ohio. It was a simple form of life in many ways, but it was nonetheless a life of privilege. I don't think I've ever really thought of myself as poor. I discovered as I became older that the Millersburg region where we lived is a part of Appalachia and got some antipoverty funds; but the people there would not have thought of themselves as poor. Another example would be the Mennonites in the Soviet Union who had to leave and who immediately created another world of privilege in Paraguay; and so I'm saying that it seems that as a people we have difficulty identifying with the oppressed. We need to grapple with this problem and get some handles on it.

John has emphasized very well the importance of justice in the Gospel and in the Christian mission. I would like to ask how and why that has not been a more explicit concept or category in our understanding of peace. We haven't dealt sufficiently with the issue of justice.

I would question, however, John's statement that the church exists for mission alone. I would see this as only one aspect of the church. The church is also concerned about the quality of its life, the fellowship. In fact, the church should be the just kingdom, the just community itself pointing the direction for a just social order.

In the discussion of self-actualization, John mentioned the importance of the ability to think and reflect critically on the relation of faith to the social order. I'm thinking about this in relation to the high school class I'm teaching, where it's so important to be able to think critically and reflectively on the scriptures in relation to our life together. In so many ways a faith that is going to be able to stand and be in conversation with rational thought in other fields needs to think critically about itself in relation to the Bible and the social order; and I felt John lifted that up very well.

Leroy Kennel: These two papers together are excellent complementations in that one asks the kind of questions that a group must always ask--Who are we? What is our mission and story?--and the other--What is our world view that informs our mission? Together, it seems to me, they supplement the previous four papers by identifying additional kinds of learning: learning by doing (particularly in relation to mission), learning in conflict (particularly between the haves and the have-nots), learning from experience, and learning with grassroots data.

Now I'm not one of the classical three minority groups. I'm not hispanic or black or female, but I too have the minority identity in my psyche. Back in Shippley High School in Nebraska, an 18-year-old Mennonite friend registered for the draft; and the superintendent got up before the assembly and said, "A very patriotic thing has happened. Clyde Swartzentruber has registered for the United States Army this morning." Clyde knew and Fred Snyder knew and I knew that Clyde was a conscientious objector. The pressure was on. Many of us have experienced a similar learning by conflict.

We are also learning from grassroots data. In my current responsibility as a coordinator for the Chicago Area Mennonites, I am working with eighteen congregations, four of which are black and four hispanic. Eleven are inner-city and seven are suburban. Only one inner-city and one suburban church have joined the hands of different racial and cultural groups. My vision for theses 9-13 of John's paper is that of joined hands. Right now we're trying to find a new coordinator for the Chicago area ministries, and it seems sometimes that we're looking for a black woman who speaks Spanish and is married to a caucasian. There are those who feel that it has to be someone who really identifies, looks like, sounds like one of the have-nots or one of the minorities. We're currently having a real challenge of communication between the inner-city churches and the suburban churches, and we're not fully trusting each other. Our problem is like the Mennonite TV-Spot of the woman who comes to pick up her husband at the factory. They embrace, they kiss, but then she slides over and he gets into the driver's seat. The call for critical examination of who is in the driver's seat is always with us, and I think it is only in the spirit of joined hands that we can learn what Rafael and John would teach us.

Alice Suderman: I wondered why I was assigned to this set of papers because my experience in cross-cultural settings has been so limited. Until my marriage I had no contact at all with other cultures. Then I made several visits to the Hopi Reservation in Arizona where my husband grew up and I had a little exposure there and another short exposure in Brazil where I visited my sister who was working in a mission. After reading these papers, one of the things that really stood out for me was the need for identification with people of another culture. I'm sure that all of us are aware that in the past our mission efforts have often failed in this regard, and we are making some real effort to correct this. An example of this kind of failure was brought home to me when I had been studying church architecture and then shortly thereafter went to visit again on the reservation in Arizona and saw the white frame church building the missionaries had built, instead of using adobe out of which everything else is built. The white frame church would have fit very well on the plains of Saskatchewan or South Dakota but hardly in that cultural setting in which that wasn't even a common kind of construction material. The need for identifying with people needs to go much deeper as Mr. Rogers pointed out, that the world view of a culture must be understood or our methodology will be wrong.

George Konrad: Rafael's paper also brought back memories from my past, and like Levi I was able to identify with his autobiographical case study in relation to my youth in a southern Manitoba village. And I wondered whether there was a way of amalgamating our history, perhaps not the ethnic cultural history unique to each of us, but the spiritual, theological history common to us all. At least I felt, "Hey, we've got the same history." That to me was amazing how from totally diverse backgrounds, we sit together at this seminar, praise the grace of God, and discover a common history. I grew up during World War II, and I remember how we were greeted on the school yard with a little ditty which ended with the words, "My main sport is killing Mennonites." When our church was burned and we were forbidden to have services in the German language, we knew there was something different about us.

Another impression I got from these papers is the way people like Rafael and John and others coming into our midst are leading the way to new directions we probably would never find on our own. I have often noticed in relation to the women's issue, for instance, how when men take the side of women, which I have tried to do again here at this Seminar, it is so often just another illustration of chauvinism; and when the white middle class person tries to help blacks or hispanics, it's so often just another illustration of paternalism, reinforcing what we're trying to overcome by the very actions we take. So perhaps the only answer is to somehow move toward each other and meet somewhere in the middle. I think that's what's happening here today, and it's exciting for me.

John said something to the effect that the mission of Christ includes the liberation of the oppressed and the empowerment of the powerless, and that apart from an identification with the powerless, the church cannot fulfill its vocation. While I have no problem with that theologically, my feet are still under this table as you notice, safely entrenched in my middle class position. What's more, I like it there. I like the safety, the security, the power. I'm not at all sure what it means to put feet to some of the concepts that I heard this afternoon. I teach in a seminary that institutionally is dependent upon the middle class social structures, and I have a hunch that most of our churches are too. What then are we perpetuating with our institutions? We think nothing of taking $100,000 for a building program from one of our rich businessmen, without asking how this money was earned and who suffered as a result. For unless I get some help from my brothers and sisters and meet them somewhere in the middle, I will probably stay right here with my feet under this table. Then merely talking about it becomes an exercise in futility.

Leland Harder: Here at this Seminary, we have certainly been working on Rafael's agenda, trying to ask what a theological curriculum would look like if we were really oriented around the missionary purpose and goal; but I also doubt whether we have really looked as seriously at John's question of what a Christian nurture would be like if it was reoriented around the concept and reality of the liberation of the oppressed. Let's turn the mike back now to Rafael and John to see whether they have any further responses to the responses.

John Rogers: I find it interesting that just about all of the responses identified oppression and powerlessness with racial and cross-cultural concerns. Personally I don't see oppression primarily in those categories. I think oppression is much deeper than that and I think the need is to get at the deeper variables of oppression, such as world view, economics, and politics. Perhaps race is the most identifiable factor, the thing we focus on; but I think it's inadequate as a basis for dealing with oppression. Also to talk about the compatability between our personal spiritual histories is inadequate if we stop with that. We've got to look at the broader questions of history. Arnoldo was getting at that this

orning when he said that we need to look at a broader history, even of minority
ersons. In the case of black persons, can you affirm slavery, Jim Crow, even
urrent history up through the present time, or do you simply dismiss all that
nd confirm only our continuity in terms of our spiritual history? We've got to
o to the broader history and commit ourselves to deal with that if we want to
alk about real identification and joining hands.

FINDINGS REPORT:
BASIC UNDERSTANDINGS OF CONGREGATIONAL NURTURE

*Laurence Martin, Herta Funk, David Helmuth,
Helen Reusser, Gordon Zook, Ross Bender*

We recognize the imperative to teach. The closing
commission of our Lord clearly focuses the mission of
the covenant community which includes the teaching ministry as one of making disciples, baptizing them in the
name of the Father, Son, and Holy Spirit, and teaching
them to observe all the things he commanded. The field
is the world and the time frame is "to the very end of
the age."

We recognize the diverse educational programs and
settings in our congregations and that it is important
they share a common vision and theology. There have
been many positive contributions of the Sunday school
movement during the past 100 years of congregational
life. One negative result has been the separation of
church service and Sunday school, of proclamation and
teaching into separate institutions many times embracing
diverse theologies and purposes. There has been the
tendency to view the Sunday school as the only institution where Christian education occurs.

We recognize the rich diversity of cultures, races,
and nationalities present in the church. The image
which provides continuity through the ages is our identity as a covenant people who share a *common salvation
story* of a creating, liberating God who is revealed in
Jesus Christ and a *common vision* of the kingdom of God,
both present and coming.

There is the need to develop a common vision and to
create flexible structures which will unify the *proclamation* (preaching, presence), *admonition* teaching,

discerning issues, discipline), *worship* (singing, prayer, praise), *fellowship* (sharing, mutual aid), and *mission* (evangelism, liberation of oppressed) functions of our congregations. The purpose of this is to allow God's Spirit to empower people individually and corporately *to grow in Christlikeness* in every area of life such that they become a visible expression of the kingdom of God. This best occurs in the context of a people of God who model and make credible the faith experience.

Growing out of our seminar on education in the congregation, we identify the following basic understandings with which to begin the task of building models of education which will help the church be faithful to its vision.

BASIC UNDERSTANDING #1. One model for education among Christians is that of a conversation (interaction) between generations in a covenant community. Full participation in a healthy functioning Christian community is an important dimension of the nurturing educative process. Through this participation God works in the formal and informal structure of community life to form personal identities and values.

IMPLICATIONS. 1. The socialization process which is described views education as happening in a holistic way. Structures need to be developed which will enhance interaction and encourage relationships across generations to develop.

2. The educational design must create those kinds of settings which best facilitate the conversation between generations. Settings in which a number of representatives from several generations are present for the conversation will be fostered. There will be both formal and informal settings and approaches in the design. Wherever feasible informal settings will be utilized since they have the advantage of freeing the flow of natural conversation between the generations in the midst of living. The equipping of the mentors for their part in the conversation

(parents, older persons, teachers) requires as disciplined an effort as that required for preparation for teaching a class in a more formal setting if they are to be able to discern and utilize the teachable moments that present themselves. Some elements in the educational settings and approaches to be included are: (a) the village circle, (b) visiting, (c) feasts, (d) camping and campfires, (e) celebrations, (f) workshops, (g) pilgrimages and storytelling, (h) apprenticeships, (i) religious dance, (j) visits by significant persons such as missionaries and church leaders, (k) house fellowships, (l) worship (congregational and family), (m) singing, (n) memorizing Scriptures.

3. God is not limited to existing structures. Free and gracious acts of God, which cannot be predicted or explained, occur in the lives of individuals and groups.

4. The congregational family is a kind of extended spiritual family and needs to be supportive of the biological family.

BASIC UNDERSTANDING #2. Intentional, deliberate education in a specified time and class setting is important to acquire adequate information, knowledge, and understanding of the Christian faith. Formal settings need to be included in an adequate Christian education design for congregations.

IMPLICATIONS. 1. Every effort should be put forth to make effective the teaching/learning programs of the church, to train teachers for their responsibilities, and to plan for life-long Christian education

2. Strong emphasis on adult education is needed.

3. Such an education program requires taking seriously the study of the Bible, theology, and history (of all groups represented)--this has implications for choice of curriculum.

4. The study of the content of the Christian faith calls for both systematic and experiential approaches with a view to building the bridge of interpretation between biblical and modern times.

5. The atmosphere of the classroom will avoid competitiveness and individualism but will instead emphasize cooperation and relationships in which teachers and students are learners together.

BASIC UNDERSTANDING #3. Worship, celebration, and proclamation within the community of faith are essential elements in congregational education. They give expression to who we are as the people of God.

IMPLICATIONS. 1. The Christian education and worship leadership of the local church needs to pay regular and deliberate attention to the educational potential of congregational worship experiences, such as (a) the Sunday morning worship hour and (b) special congregational events.

2. Worship, proclamation, and celebration should consider the involvement of children and youth, as well as adults.

3. Pastors and worship leaders need to be aware of the agenda and content of church school classes so that familiar images, references, music, etc., can be incorporated in corporate worship settings.

BASIC UNDERSTANDING #4. The telling and retelling of the salvation story by the believing community and its representatives is an important way in which the revelation of God's will is communicated in the Christian education process. This includes reflecting on the meaning of the story as well as the process of remembering the past with the view to applying insights in new ways to the present and in giving hope for the future.

IMPLICATIONS. 1. The Bible is our sourcebook of telling the salvation story.

2. God's saving work continues even in our time.

3. Proclamation and worship are essential ways of telling and retelling the salvation story.

4. The use of ritual and rites of passage can be an educational method in storytelling and remembering

5. Reading the Bible in a systematic way, both personally and corporately, helps us to remember the salvation story in its entirety.

BASIC UNDERSTANDING #5. The primary responsibility for the total well being of children, including nurture in the Christian faith, lies with the home. Through the congregation parents are assisted in their responsibility

IMPLICATIONS. 1. The Christian family should not abdicate its responsibility for the nurture of its children in the Christian faith.

2. The church needs to be called to a renewed awareness of being a spiritual family called to provide support and resources for the nurturing functions of the home.

3. The educational settings of the church must take the family unit into account in planning for congregational educational experiences.

4. A theology and practice of the congregation as a spiritual family to all members needs to be fostered in such a way as not to replace the biological family, but to make a unique contribution to members who have families.

5. Where parents are not available to participate in complementary efforts to nurture children, special assistance may be needed.

BASIC UNDERSTANDING #6. The life, faith, and relationships of the teacher and the Christian community are of

crucial significance to the learer. Jesus provides
models for the church's teaching ministry today.

IMPLICATIONS. 1. Teacher training based on a study
of Jesus as a teacher takes note of (a) settings used,
(b) storytelling methods, (c) dialogue methods, (d)
prayer, (e) intimate knowledge and relationship with
student.

2. The self-understanding of Jesus as a teacher
included being (a) an *example* to groups being taught,
(b) a *prophet* or *revealer* of God proclaiming the
kingdom of God, (c) a *re-visionist* who re-visions the
tradition in new ways for the current situation (a
teacher is an agent of change), (d) a *priest* who
lives on behalf of another, and (e) a *king* who reveals the kingdom of God.

3. Teachers are crucial: as examples and models
equipped with values important to the community such
as love, care, etc.

BASIC UNDERSTANDING #7. Adult education prepares people
individually and collectively as a part of the Body of
Christ to be an effective Christian Presence in the
world, where God is already at work. God invites people
to be part of his plan to "unite all things in heaven
and earth under one head, even Christ."

IMPLICATIONS. 1. To be an effective Christian Presence means that one enters life prepared to be
totally involved as God through the Holy Spirit
directs.

2. Adult education has an element of discipleship
and mission connected with it.

BASIC UNDERSTANDING #8. The Holy Spirit gives gifts to
the Body of Christ and the role of the Holy Spirit is
vital and foundational to all that happens in Christian
education. The Holy Spirit prepares the learner to
receive new insights, motivates the learner to seek

changes in attitude and behavior, and equips the Christian educator for the task of effective learning.

IMPLICATIONS. 1. Spiritual life disciplines (Bible
reading, prayer, meditation, etc.) are an essential
area of preparation for the Christian educator and
an area of growth and development for all learners.

2. The development of resources for the intentional and systematic use of spiritual life disciplines is essential to an effective program of
Christian education.

BASIC UNDERSTANDING #9. On the basis of the Great Commission, the evangelizing and teaching ministries of the
church are interrelated. Christian nurture and instruction usually both precede and follow a conversion experience, in the first case preparing the way, in the latter
building upon it.

IMPLICATIONS. 1. Discipling as an act of evangelizing has both educational and conversional elements.

2. The goal of conversion is transformed lives
which individually and corporately as the Body of
Christ are an expression of the kingdom of God
values and a resulting lifestyle.

3. Christian educators need to call persons to
new levels of conversion amidst the crises of our
lives, especially in these turbulent times which
demand that we pass through the ordeal of a new
interpretation of faith.

4. While Christian educators often work particularly with the process of intellectual conversion,
we nevertheless must keep the whole person in focus
and be willing to be instruments through which the
Holy Spirit can invite persons to experience a
transformation which touches every area of their
life.

5. The teacher's concern is not only with the process of conversion in students, but with the process in his or her life.

6. Just as the revelation of God's will was made known to humankind when they were prepared to receive it, so certain insights and commitments may not be fully comprehended until a learner is developmentally and emotionally prepared to receive and make them.

BASIC UNDERSTANDING #10. God wills that congregations find ways to work toward greater unity of vision and theology in all aspects of church life including education, proclamation, worship, and mission. Appropriate educational approaches will need to be used to foster and express this unity.

IMPLICATIONS. 1. New ways to study, plan, administer, and evaluate congregational education programs need to be developed so that a common vision emerges.

2. For effective congregational education to occur, pastors and leadership teams in congregations must be aware of the educational dimension of life in the congregation. They need to be aware of the educative potential in all that occurs in congregational life.

[The following issues emerged, but were not brought to closure. Readers are asked to continue the discussion.]

ISSUE #1. All educating arises from or reflects a given world view. Therefore, the educator must be aware of and critical of his or her world view and be wary of the limits that personally held world views place on both teachers and students. Teachers must see themselves as partners with their students in the educating process as together they live in the world and the kingdom where God is acting to accomplish (God's) purposes.

POSSIBLE IMPLICATIONS. Historically there has been

an assumption that teaching was an activity of transmission of meaning or interpretation, but this is not
a possibility for any person. Meaning or interpretation is a function of the interrelationship of
ideas and experiences in the complex interaction of
an individual...and the meaning held by one person
cannot be transferred, with its whole set of complex
relationships, to another person. The teacher can
confront a student with ideas to which he must react,
but the reaction cannot be controlled. The teacher
can question and challenge each articipation of meaning; but if the answer is determined a priority, the
process of thinking is truncated. There can be no
necessary response, either in tempo or intensity.
The distinctive contribution of the teacher is the
presentation of another perspective in the light of
which the student may reflect upon the meanings he
already holds (see Gordon Chamberlin, *Toward a
Phenomenology of Education* (Philadelphia: The
Westminster Press, 1969).

2. Failure to recognize or accept this reality
(and its implications for communal and societal
transcendence) may lead to attempts to limit the
experiences and the thought processes of the learners
We begin to see our experiences and insights as
normative. The end is closed-mindedness and a closin
of identity, which, in turn, may hinder movement
toward the realization of the kingdom of God.

ISSUE #2. The reference and direction for developing
Christian congregational vision and educational models
comes from the Bible, from Christian history, and from
Spirit-directed consultation of brothers and sisters.
Methods and models other than these are appropriate as
long as they do not violate the basic values of Christian experience.

POSSIBLE IMPLICATIONS. (1) Models of education which
value personal relationships and respect of individua
choice are acceptable. (2) Methods which are propa-
gandist in nature and discourage the development of
self-awareness are usually inappropriate.

RESPONSES OF THE CONGREGATIONAL LISTENING TEAM

Marvin Hostetler: *Beth and I want to preface our report with two comments. One is that we are not typical grassroots people from our churches. I am a seminary student and Beth is a part-time professor elementary education; and that's not quite grassroots. I think grassroots people from our churches would have left this seminar-workshop after the first session.*

Nor is Berkey Avenue Fellowship exactly a typical church in our Conferences. I'll give you a little history for that. We have a history of only three years. We started in July 1979 with Sunday evening meetings on a weekly basis at Bethany Christian High School. Then we moved to Sunday morning services at the Mennonite Mutual Aid building on North Main. That shift alone meant a growth from thirty-five persons to around sixty. By the time we left MMA we were up to 110 persons, which has since doubled to 220. The people of the Bethany days are known as the 'pioneers.' The people of the MMA days are the "homesteaders," meeting in the Upper Room, and the people of the lower room at MMA and at our present new church building are the "sinners." We've come from a diverse background of Old Mennonites, GCs, Church of the Brethren, Methodist, Apostolic Christian, Catholic, Assembly of God, and unchurched pagan. This has resulted in a bit of unsettledness in the expectations for worship format. Neighborhood kids are starting to come, although we are making no particular effort to reach them. We are a unique congregation in that the impetus for who we are and what we do comes more from the people rather than from the pastor pulling teeth to get us going. He guides us rather than feeds us. The originals plus the pioneers were the ones who worked on design of the building. We also said from the beginning that 250 would be maximum, after which we would divide into two congregations. We are nearly there already without having an adequate vision for what we were working towards. Small groups and home fellowships are an important part of our nurture program, and 80 percent of our adults participate.

One of the issues we are working on is intergenerational education. When we were strangers to each other, the nurture committee assigned persons to groups, in each of which a teacher was chosen. Each adult group was also a parent group for their children, and there was supposed to be interaction between the adult groups and the kids' group. This didn't quite work because the nurture committee failed to communicate what we desired to happen in these nurture groups. Now we are struggling with how worship and nurture relate, with how children are to be involved in worship. We have them read Scripture, take up the offering, and participate in a children's story time.

Our biggest question for next year is vision. Who are we as a people? What are the minimum requirements for being a part of our church? What does it mean to be a disciple of Jesus? What kind of mission do we as Berkey Avenue Fellowship see that the west Goshen neighborhood could use? Who are the people of west Goshen who would match up with the people of Berkey Avenue?

Beth Berry: *As Marv and I talked about our assignment, we thought we'd like to include some critique of the methodology we have experienced in this seminar and to express the way we have felt about a lot of the ideas expressed here. As we sat down at supper last night before the assumptions were distributed, we found that the issues we listed as grassroots issues from the inputs and discussions were by and large what came out in the list of assumptions that were presented last night. We felt positive about that. We felt that the approach of this Conference, coming in as observers as we did, was definitely what Peter Erb terms a "lettered approach," while most of the people in our congregations are not lettered although they are literate. They don't read a lot of books, at least not in depth; but they watch a lot of TV and movies. We thought that perhaps there is something to be said for the medieval model that was presented and that needs to be remembered in that it relates to our work of Christian education. He mentioned that the*

medieval person "read" art, architecture, pictures, statues, sacred objects, etc.
Maybe we need to consider that approach even in the way we structure a conference designed to reexamine the meaning and method of Christian education. We
were overwhelmed by the amount of intellectualizing, and we began to imagine some
alternate methods that might have been planned. If you are indeed all committed
to the importance of Christian education, you could have done your homework ahead
of time, read the papers in advance, and devoted five minutes to the presenter's
highlight review. Then the group could have been helped to highlight the important concepts in each paper by simulations of various kinds, such as a dramati-
zation of the village circle from Janzen's paper, or a video-tape of a congregational group working at nurturing through singing, admonition, and teaching
according to the Colossians text cited by Brunk. Or there might have been a slide
presentation of a medieval cathedral with its "principle of reserve" from Erb's
paper. Then could follow the responses with more time for discussion and brain-
storming, which we found quite helpful, except that the time for it was too short.
Or perhaps it would have been good to move all these tables to the walls and
listened to an inner circle of Sunday school teachers and parents talking about
Christian education in their congregation from their perspective.

I realize the importance of philosophy and theory and vision. I don't mean
to knock that at all. As an educator and teacher, I am aware of the need for that;
but I think it becomes a question of correspondence between theory and life
situation. Do we set the vision here and then try later to discover ways to get
it down to the grassroots, or do we explore the grassroots and try to see how we
can lift that up into a vision of nurturing the faith, and how we correlate these
two things?

At Berkey Avenue Fellowship, we have a sharing time each Sunday morning; and
people get up and express a need they have, a thanksgiving they feel, a response
to the sermon input or to other facets of the worship. Although the children are
not the ones who are standing up and speaking, we observe them absorbing and learning from this method as persons share with each other, persons who can tell each
other their hurts and praises and can thank God for themselves and for each other.

Also, our people would not respond very well to a formal quarter of study on
Mennonite history and theology, but they would respond to well told stories,
if they could incorporate history and theology; and they would absorb it that way,
utilizing teachable moments in informal situations. We have a "nurture time" at
Berkey Avenue. We use that nomenclature in our Sunday school, calling it "nurture
time." A question I feel needs to be raised from the grassroots level about
teaching in formal settings is the question of indoctrination versus teaching. We
have been talking about teaching as relational and exemplar and inquiry-evoking
rather than the fund of knowledge. I feel that many parents are opting for an
indoctrination approach because they do not really want to know and to see or to
hear the kind of cognitive knowledge you have been teaching here these days.
Again, as I said before, I find myself sympathetic with what I've heard you say,
I don't believe that's where the majority of the people in our churches are at.
We find it difficult to find time even for our nurture committee to meet to plan
all those good things. One of our good people on the nurture committee mentioned
last week during basketball tournament time that she had gone to eleven basketball
games in one week. That's just the nitty-gritty of what's happening in our time.
How do we recover time for what we view as important? How do we change our view
of what's important?

PLENARY DISCUSSION

Leland Harder: Beth and Marv, you have fulfilled very well the observer
reporter role we assigned to you. Your candid confrontative sharing of impressions
of our seminar in your perspective as members and leaders of a diverse and inno-
vative fellowship is much appreciated, and we will try hard not to be defensive
but rather to benefit as we respond now to your responses.

Don Miller: I really appreciate their comments. Our hindsight is always better than our foresight, and these are helpful suggestions. I don't know the intentions of the Institute of Mennonite Studies, but it seems to me that a good foundation has been laid for some follow-up workshops along the lines they have described.

Helen Reusser: I resonate with that. I wasn't ready to leave after the first session, but yesterday I could have. It got a little too heavy, although I appreciate the background and understanding I have gleaned from the presenters who have much more knowledge and training than I do. I work with eighty some congregations in Ontario, and what these people have said is right on. It's so important to keep in touch with where people are at and try to move them to where we want them to be, although that's a difficult task. But to me, that's Christian education: moving people from where they are to where we'd like them to be. We can dream and brainstorm all we want, but we have to know where people are and start from there. When I plan workshops, I don't come with some preconceived notion that I am going to foist on them, which is the way we plan so often.

Paul Unruh: I would like to get a word in quick before the presenters and planners of this seminar go out and hang themselves. Those of you who know me well know that 95 percent of me is farm boy, and occasionally I take a peek into the academic world. I really wonder whether the listening team respondents understood the objectives of this seminar. I don't think these papers were ever meant to be the whole show. One of the things that I need as a grassroots person is precisely this kind of a seminar. Last night when I called my wife to take care of a little piece of business, she asked how it was going. I said, "Well, I'm about seven feet tall because I've had to stretch for three days, and I'm not accustomed to that." And so I would make very few apologies for the academic atmosphere to which we've been subjected here.

Waldemar Janzen: At the risk of running counter to much of what the listening team said, I would like to warn against what sounds to me like some grassroots romanticism. I think of many people in Paraguay in the Chaco where they have few trained leaders and where they cry out for literature, for material to read, for trained teachers, etc. I spoke with someone who came from the Soveit Union recently, an elderly gentleman; and I asked him what the church there needs most. And he said books on church history and leadership training. They don't have many people like John Rogers and Rafael Falcon, and they would be glad if they had more trained leaders like them. Most of us around these tables have university degrees, and we are reacting to our riches, whipping ourselves for not being grassroots. We quite rightly don't want to be top heavy; but I think we also need places like this where we can rethink our teaching ministries; and if you take seminars like this away, we will get back to a situation of mental and spiritual poverty.

We certainly need to listen to the grassroots for cues as to how to communicate and relate to people where they're at, but the grassroots is not the place for which we can look for revelation. Where does the real truth come from? From the unsophisticated utterances of those we call grassroots? Surely, God can speak through anyone and everyone, but the core of the truth that we have to communicate is not in asking the educated or sophisticated or grassroots, but in Scripture; and there have been moments here during this conference when I felt that the canon was tilting a bit in the direction of what the grassroots feel over against what the Scripture teaches.

Beth Berry: I think maybe I would like to repeat one sentence that I did say, and I mean it, that I realize the importance of formulating a philosophy and a vision of Christian nurture; and I don't think we meant to say "no" to that when we said that you've got to listen to what the little guys say when you envision your model. We were just making a plea that there be a meeting of minds and a working together, not either one telling the other what is the revelation of God.

Leland Harder: I think we are ready for the next conversation on strategy. At this point I think we will get our coffee and tea. Let's really try to bring them back to the tables, so that we can go on with our work.